Tom Kerridge's
Best Ever Dishes

Tom Kerridge's
Best Ever Dishes

A.

To the biggest support in my life, my best mate and the foundation on which everything is built, my lovely wife Bef ;) Also, to the three daft dogs... love you!

I consider myself a very lucky man. I spend my life with people I love, making great food for customers who really seem to appreciate it. There's not a day I drive to work at my pub, The Hand & Flowers, when I don't feel excited about what's going to happen next.

Even though it's really hard work, I try to make each dish as good as I can; my own, personal, best ever. And that's what I want to share with you in this book: my special take on familiar dishes like tomato soup, lasagne, shepherd's pie, rice pudding and chocolate tart, as well as more exotic delights. I'm showing you all of the tweaks, tricks and techniques I've learned over the past twenty years or so, to transform the everyday into the spectacular. I've pumped up the flavour and, I hope, given these recipes a whole new lease of life.

I wasn't the most obvious person to run a two-Michelin-starred kitchen. I grew up in Gloucester and went to an all-boys comprehensive school, which I loved. Not so much the classes as what was in between them – hanging out with my mates, having a laugh. My mum called it 'the school of life'.

From when I was eleven, Mum brought up my little brother and me on her own. She had two jobs: working for the council in the day then at a pub in the evening, so often I made the tea. It was nothing posh – beans on toast, fish finger sandwiches, that sort of thing. Then one day I put a bit of curry powder in the beans to make it different. Every Wednesday I made a bolognaise sauce from scratch for Thursday night's tea. Mum would supervise at first but then I just got on with it myself. It wasn't a life where you would bake a cake and lick the beaters; it was proper dinner.

That bolognaise was my first kind of interesting cooking I suppose, but I didn't catch the bug properly until I was about eighteen and I got my first real job in the kitchen at Calcot Manor in Tetbury. The moment I went into the kitchen, I knew it was the place for me. At that point, it wasn't even about the food. It was that atmosphere, the camaraderie where everyone works hard but you can have a laugh too – mess about, have a few jokes with the naughty boys like I did at school, plus the flames and knives! But I liked the sense of order too, the discipline and hierarchy of us all pulling together to get the job done, and that's never left me.

When I was twenty-one, I went to London. I knew that was where I wanted to work and it was a great time to be there. The restaurant scene was becoming really exciting. Marco Pierre White was cooking with three stars, Nico Ladenis was running Chez Nico, Gordon Ramsay was getting going at Aubergine.

I got a job at the Capital Hotel, which had a serious kitchen. I was determined to learn as much as I could – to put in the hard graft, to develop my love of food and understanding of it.

I learned the most important lesson: that ingredients and how to source the best is where you do all of the really hard work. Since then, all my kitchens and dishes have been ingredient led. Learning how to cook, whether you're in a professional kitchen or cooking for your family and mates at home, is just a process of knowing how to get the best out of your ingredients; how to create the most intense flavours. I don't think of myself as an artist, I see myself as a craftsman – someone who's learned his trade, knows his ingredients and what he wants to do with them.

I remember when I was just starting out, I made a garlic sauce and my mum said, 'This really tastes of garlic!' I was so disappointed, like it was a bad thing, but then I realised – hang on, that's what I want! Cooking is sometimes just a process of ensuring things really taste of themselves.

I like big flavours. I like getting the balance of taste and texture just right – sweet, acid, crunch, silkiness. And I'm obsessed with seasoning. You'll see as you go through this book how much I like curing, brining and salting, rubs and marinades. I take every chance I can to add some extra flavour.

I hope you won't be nervous about getting stuck in. None of the recipes here are particularly difficult. Some of them might take a little time, but a lot of that is usually the dish sitting in the fridge or oven letting the ingredients do the work for you as they mingle and develop into something lovely.

And most of all, I hope you have fun. When I'm in the kitchen I'm confident, I'm smiling, I'm laughing. And I was like that even before I had the skills to back it up! Put in enough care, give it your best go, and who cares if your dish doesn't look absolutely perfect? It'll still taste brilliant. With practice, you can always improve technique. Cook with love and I promise you that'll shine through on the plate.

equipment & ingredients

Before you get cracking, a bit of housekeeping. I don't want to get all cheffy on you, but there are some bits of kit I rely on every day and use in some of the recipes here. None of them are very expensive or elaborate, but I guarantee they'll make your life easier, for these recipes and for all of your cooking, so they're worth the investment. For fine slicing of ingredients, such as coleslaws and other salads, a Japanese mandolin will give you perfectly shredded veg in no time. I like a Microplane-type grater too. They're brilliant for getting the finest possible texture from garlic, ginger, citrus zests and nutmeg. For spice rubs and curry powder, a pestle and mortar or a spice grinder will

help you produce great texture for very little outlay. I also think a meat mincer is a useful addition to any kitchen. It means you can grind meat to exactly the grade of coarseness you want and you can mince specific cuts of meat for terrines and sauces. An instant-read thermometer will definitely earn its keep in your kitchen: use it for deep-frying, judging whether meat is done and making perfect custards and sauces. Lastly, a blowtorch, which I use in several of these recipes. Apart from being great fun and easy to operate, they're brilliant for adding colour to roasts and for charring things like lemon slices for the most incredible garnish. Just make sure that the ingredient you're flaming is on a heatproof surface, such as a metal tray, before you fire up the blowtorch.

Finally, a few words about ingredients and their preparation. Throughout this book, in the lists of ingredients, all of the fruit and veg are medium-sized and washed and peeled unless otherwise stated. Lemons and other citrus fruits are unwaxed ideally, but if you can only get the waxed kind give them a good scrub under a hot tap before using the zest. All eggs are large. Milk, yoghurt and other dairy products are lovely full-fat versions. Butter is unsalted, and salt is ordinary table salt unless I specify the flaky sea stuff because its texture is an important part of the dish. Cracked black pepper is required for the punch it gives a dish – you can find it in supermarkets. For general seasoning, use freshly ground pepper. I always make my own stock but I appreciate this isn't possible all the time. So if you haven't got any home-made stock in the freezer, you can substitute my version with a good-quality shop-bought variety of whichever type is called for in the recipe.

And now you're ready to get started. As much as I want you to enjoy my best ever dishes, I hope you'll take them, play with them, adapt them and make some best ever dishes of your own.

starters

You might be a bit surprised to hear this from me, but I think one of the most important things about the beginning of a meal is to keep it simple if you need to.

There's no shame in putting out a board covered with fantastic salami and a bowl of pickles, or a plate of lovely radishes with some great butter and flaky sea salt. Who wouldn't love that?

At the starter stage it's as if you're taking your guests by the hand and leading them into the meal, showing them where you're going to go. You set the mood for the rest of the dinner, so if you're calm and confident, they'll relax, all ready to have a brilliant time. If you're a frazzled mess trying to do ten things at once while the smoke alarm goes off and the dog runs off with the steak, what do you think your guests are going to remember?

A three-course meal can be a lot of work. I know – I serve dozens of them nearly every day, and I have a full brigade to back me up! So in this chapter I've included some of my favourite starters, such as the Ham butter and the Spiced lamb terrine, which you can make well ahead so they're ready when you want to sit down to dinner. Even the things you have to serve immediately, like the Wok-steamed cockles or Scallops and brown shrimp, are easy if you do all of the preparation ahead and then just steam or bake them at the last minute.

Of course, having said all that, sometimes I can't resist a showstopper – a bit of drama, like the Ham fritters with cheese fondue, which you serve inside a baked onion. The secret here is to make sure that for the main course and pudding you've chosen things that you can mostly prepare in advance so you're not giving yourself too much work on the day. That way, you can relax, enjoy your dinner and, most of all, the company of your friends.

Corn on the cob with lots of melting butter is one of the big joys of summer. But sometimes you can make a good thing better, right? Here, I've combined the sweetness of the corn kernels with a bit of heat from the chilli and spices, and have added lovely caramelised onions.

Spiced roast corn on the cob & burnt onion ketchup

SERVES 4

100g softened butter
1 teaspoon smoked paprika
1 teaspoon dried sage
1 teaspoon chilli flakes
1 teaspoon garlic powder
1 teaspoon cracked
   black pepper
1 teaspoon salt
4 corn cobs, husk
   and silk removed

For the burnt onion ketchup
2–3 tablespoons vegetable oil
3 onions, halved and
   thinly sliced
150ml white wine vinegar
50g dark muscovado sugar
1 tablespoon Worcestershire
   sauce
2 dried bay leaves
3 garlic cloves, grated
1 tablespoon chopped
   salted anchovies

First make the ketchup. Warm a large, non-stick frying pan over a high heat and drizzle in a little of the oil. You will need to cook the onions in batches so that they caramelise properly. Add a small handful of the onions and fry until they go brown and slightly charred – you are looking for the sweet taste of hot-dog onions! When cooked, set each batch aside in a bowl and continue with the rest.

Put the vinegar, sugar, Worcestershire sauce and bay leaves into a medium-sized saucepan and heat, stirring to dissolve the sugar. Bring to the boil and add the garlic and the sautéed onions. Leave on a low heat to simmer gently for 25 minutes until the onions are soft. Stir from time to time. Remove the bay leaves and stir in the anchovies.

Place the mixture in a blender or food processor and process until smooth; you may need to add a little water. Next, pass it through a fine sieve into a small bowl and put a piece of cling film directly on the top to stop a skin forming. Leave to cool at room temperature. When cool, keep in the fridge until needed. This will keep, sealed and refrigerated, for a few days if required.

Preheat the oven to 200°C/Gas Mark 6.

For the corn, beat together the butter, paprika, sage, chilli flakes, garlic powder, pepper and salt in a small bowl and spread the mixture all over the corn. Wrap each cob tightly in tin foil. Place on a baking tray and roast in the oven for 20–25 minutes until the corn is tender.

Serve the pieces of corn in their foil, with bowls of the burnt onion ketchup on the side.

These are a great lunch dish, either on their own as a starter or served on the side of a more substantial main course. Blue cheese and bacon are natural partners for each other, giving a big, salty kick that is softened by the cool, crisp lettuce and celery sticks.

Cheesy baked potato skins

4 baking potatoes
Olive oil, for drizzling
8 rashers of thick-cut pancetta
2 cos lettuces, leaves separated
   and roughly chopped
4 celery sticks, tough strings
   removed, thinly sliced,
   leaves reserved for garnish
2 tablespoons chopped
   celery leaves
2 tablespoons chopped chives
Smoked paprika, for dusting
   (optional)

For the cheesy dressing
250g crème fraîche
200g Roquefort cheese,
   crumbled
100g mayonnaise
1 tablespoon Dijon mustard
Few splashes of Tabasco sauce
Salt and freshly ground
   black pepper

Preheat the oven to 180°C/Gas Mark 4.
.....

Place the potatoes in the oven on a baking tray and bake for 1¼ hours, until the potatoes are crisp on the outside and cooked in the middle. Remove from the oven but leave the oven on. Leave the potatoes to cool for 10–15 minutes.
.....

Cut the potatoes in half lengthways and scoop out the flesh, trying not to break the skins. (You can keep the scooped-out potato to make potato pancakes for breakfast.) Put the hollowed-out potato skins back on the baking tray, drizzle with a little oil and return them to the oven for about 15–20 minutes, until they are crisp and brown. Remove from the oven and keep to one side.
.....

For the dressing, gently fold together the crème fraîche, Roquefort and mayonnaise in a bowl. Stir in the mustard and Tabasco and season to taste to form a lovely, rich cheesy dressing.
.....

Place the pancetta under a hot grill until crisp, then set aside.
.....

Combine the lettuce and celery in a large bowl then add the cheesy dressing and stir together. Place the rashers of crisp pancetta in the baked potato skins, then spoon the lettuce mixture on top. Cover each one with some chopped celery leaves and chives and a dusting of paprika, if you like.

This is a combination of smoky fish, crunchy vegetables, soured cream and a nice little boozy punch from the vodka. Altogether it's a great dish full of tempting, contrasting colours and textures.

Smoked haddock with beetroot slaw

SERVES 4

150ml white wine
150ml water
1 teaspoon whole
    black peppercorns
2 bay leaves
2 cloves
2 x 350g smoked haddock
    fillets, skinned and pin
    bones removed

For the beetroot slaw
2 large, raw red beetroots,
    peeled and coarsely grated
2 red onions, thinly sliced
200g red cabbage, tough core
    removed, thinly sliced
2 tablespoons flaky sea salt
3 tablespoons mayonnaise
2 tablespoons prepared
    English mustard
2 tablespoons
    chopped chervil
1 Bramley apple,
    cored but unpeeled

For the vodka crème fraîche
200g crème fraîche
50ml vodka
Finely grated zest of 1 lime
2 teaspoons cracked
    black pepper
Pinch of salt
1 tablespoon finely
    chopped dill

First make the beetroot slaw. Mix all of the raw vegetables together in a bowl and sprinkle over the flaky sea salt. Mix together with your hands and leave for 10 minutes for the vegetables to macerate and soften. Place a colander in the sink and tip the vegetables into it to drain. Rinse under cold, running water for 2–3 minutes. Pat dry on a clean tea towel and squeeze out any excess moisture.
.....

In a large bowl, mix together the mayonnaise, mustard and chervil. Add the drained vegetables to the bowl. Grate the Bramley apple on to a clean tea towel with a coarse grater. Squeeze out the excess moisture then add it to the bowl. Mix all of the ingredients together and keep in the fridge, covered in cling film, until needed, for up to 1 hour.
.....

Place the crème fraîche, vodka, lime zest, black pepper and salt in a bowl and whisk until you get the thickness of clotted cream. Fold in the dill and transfer to a clean bowl. Cover with cling film and keep in the fridge until needed.
.....

For the haddock, pour the white wine and water into a shallow sauté pan or large frying pan and add the peppercorns, bay leaves and cloves. Bring to a gentle simmer. Cut the haddock fillets in half widthways so you have four pieces. Carefully place them in the simmering liquor. Gently poach the haddock for 8 minutes, basting with the liquor until cooked. Remove the fillets from the pan and serve immediately, with the vodka crème fraîche and beetroot slaw.

Smoked eel has such a fantastic taste and is one of life's luxuries. If you haven't tried it before, get some! You could think of it as slightly fishy pork belly or bacon. It has a great meat-like texture and goes so well with pear or apple. Eel should, however, be considered a treat. Its sustainability is in question and you need to be careful about how you source it. Check online if in doubt.

Smoked eel with pear, lime & Szechuan pepper

SERVES 4

2 ripe pears
8 x 35g smoked eel fillets
1 Chinese leaf lettuce, sliced

For the dressing
3 tablespoons rapeseed oil, the best quality you can find
Juice and finely grated zest of 2 limes
1 tablespoon dark soy sauce
1 tablespoon sesame oil
2 teaspoons Szechuan pepper, crushed

For the crème fraîche
150g crème fraîche
4 tablespoons freshly grated horseradish
Juice of ½ lemon
1 tablespoon icing sugar
½ teaspoon wasabi paste

Preheat the oven to 140°C/Gas Mark 1.

. . . . .

Start by making the dressing. In a bowl, mix together the rapeseed oil, lime juice and zest, soy sauce, sesame oil and Szechuan pepper.

. . . . .

In a separate bowl, whisk together the crème fraîche, horseradish, lemon juice, icing sugar and wasabi until the mixture thickens.

. . . . .

Quarter the pears and remove the core and pips. Slice the pears into nice, evenly sized pieces and divide between four plates.

. . . . .

Put the smoked eel fillets on to a baking sheet and warm them in the oven for about 2–3 minutes only. Remove and place them on the pears. Scatter some of the Chinese leaf on top then trickle over the lime dressing. Dollop a spoon of the crème fraîche mix on to each plate and serve immediately. Simple!

The taste of a fresh sardine is the ultimate summer flavour for me, and pairing it with a slightly spiced tomato dressing is the best combination. This is perfect outdoor finger food served straight from the grill or just off the barbie. You'll only need half the tomato sauce for this recipe but the leftover sauce will keep in the fridge for three days and is delicious used to dress pasta or in a chilli con carne.

Sardines with warm tomato sauce

SERVES 4

12 fresh sardines,
   gutted and scaled
Olive oil, for greasing
   the baking tray
Flaky sea salt

For the tomato sauce
1kg ripe plum tomatoes,
   halved lengthways
50g caster sugar
100ml extra virgin olive oil
1 Spanish onion, diced
4 garlic cloves, minced
2 red chillies, diced –
   seeds and all
Pinch of saffron threads
100ml white wine
75ml red wine vinegar
1 teaspoon smoked paprika

For the tomato salsa
1 red onion, finely diced
1 ripe plum tomato,
   finely diced
1 small red chilli, finely
   diced – seeds and all
1 small red pepper, cored,
   deseeded and finely diced
4 tablespoons chopped
   basil leaves, plus a little
   more for garnishing
2 tablespoons chopped
   chervil, plus a little
   more for garnishing

Preheat the oven to 180°C/Gas Mark 4. First, make the tomato sauce. Place the tomatoes in a roasting tin, sprinkle them with the sugar and roast for 20–30 minutes until they are slightly caramelised and very soft. Set aside.

.....

Warm the olive oil in a large, heavy-bottomed saucepan over a medium heat. Add the onion and garlic and cook, stirring from time to time, until the onions are soft and have taken on a bit of colour – about 15 minutes. Stir in the chillies and saffron and cook for a further 1–2 minutes. Add the wine, vinegar and smoked paprika. Scrape in the roasted tomatoes and any juice that has accumulated in the tin. Cook gently on a low heat for 40–45 minutes, stirring from time to time. Season then purée in a blender or food processor until very smooth. Pass through a fine sieve into a clean bowl.

.....

Just before you are ready to serve, put the sardines on to an oiled baking tray and season with the flaky sea salt. Place under a very hot grill until the skin crisps and begins to char – this will take 3–5 minutes – then flip the sardines over to warm the other side.

.....

While the fish are grilling, mix together all the ingredients for the salsa in a small bowl and warm up half the tomato sauce (cover and chill the remainder for another time – it will keep for up to 3 days).

.....

Place the sardines in a warmed serving dish. Either spoon the salsa and tomato sauce over separately and scatter over the basil and chervil, or mix everything together before pouring over the fish. Serve immediately.

Boom! This is a great centrepiece starter, big on visual impact and even bigger on taste. The pastries can be made up to four hours in advance then stored in the fridge until you're ready to cook them. After you've made these once, you'll start to think of all sorts of different fillings so do change the ingredients around to suit your own tastes.

Scallops & brown shrimp baked in seaweed filo

80g samphire, picked over
200g butter
3 sheets of nori seaweed
1 x 250g packet of filo pastry
2 spring onions, trimmed and finely sliced
1 tablespoon finely chopped coriander
4 very large scallops, removed from their shells (keep the shells), corals trimmed and cleaned – you can ask the fishmonger to do this for you
100g peeled brown shrimp
Juice of ½ lemon
Flaky sea salt, to finish
Freshly ground black pepper

Place the samphire in a bowl, cover with boiling water from the kettle and leave for 5 minutes to blanch and clean. Drain in a colander then rinse under cold, running water. Pat dry and set aside.

. . . . .

To make the filo layers, melt the butter in a saucepan on a low heat and set aside half in a bowl. Grind the nori to a rough powder in a spice grinder or with a pestle and mortar. Lay a sheet of filo out on a clean, dry work surface and brush with melted butter. Dust the filo with a layer of the ground seaweed. Place a second sheet of filo on top. Brush with butter and dust with seaweed. Then place a third piece of filo on top. Work quickly so the fragile filo doesn't dry out.

. . . . .

Place a thin layer of samphire, a pinch of the spring onion and a pinch of coriander in each scallop shell, followed by 25g of the brown shrimp. Place a scallop and its coral on top and then add a little lemon juice, trickle over 25ml of the reserved butter from the bowl and season with a little black pepper.

. . . . .

Cut the filo and seaweed layer into a rough circle, brush with a little more melted butter from the pan, then place the filo over the top of the scallop shell. Stick it down underneath the scallop shell with a little more melted butter. Repeat with the other 3 scallops. Chill until needed – these can be made up to 4 hours in advance.

. . . . .

Preheat the oven to 190°C/Gas Mark 5. Remove the shells from the fridge and brush the filo pastry with water. Sprinkle on some flaky sea salt. Put four ramekins on to a large baking tray and place the scallop shells on top – this will stop the rounded bottom of the shell rolling around. Alternatively, you can nestle the shells in small piles of flaky sea salt to keep them stable. Place the tray in the oven and bake for 15 minutes, until the filo is browned and crisp. Remove from the oven and serve immediately.

This is a very quick and easy dish – the trick is to prep all the vegetables first so they can go straight into the wok and then it's ready in no time at all. The cockles work well on their own as a starter or as an accompaniment to steamed sea bass or stirred through noodles as a more substantial main course.

Wok-steamed cockles with ginger & pak choi

SERVES 4 (OR 2 AS A MAIN COURSE)

1kg fresh cockles in
  their shells
2 tablespoons vegetable oil
3 garlic cloves, thinly sliced
2 red chillies, finely chopped
  – seeds and all
1 teaspoon chilli flakes
3cm knob of fresh ginger,
  peeled and grated
  to a pulp
2 tablespoons dark soy sauce
1–2 heads of pak choi,
  leaves separated
1 bunch of Chinese
  broccoli, trimmed
  and leaves separated
1 tablespoon sesame oil
2 tablespoons chopped
  coriander

First, clean the cockles carefully. Discard any cockles with broken shells or any open ones that don't snap shut when tapped. Wash under cold, running water to remove any grit or dirt. Don't cut corners here – run the water long enough to clean them properly. This can sometimes take up to an hour. Drain in a colander.
. . . . .

Place the wok on the hob and warm over a high heat. Add the vegetable oil then throw in the garlic, fresh chilli and chilli flakes. Cook for about a minute until the garlic starts to colour and then stir in the ginger.
. . . . .

Add the cleaned cockles, stirring all the time. Pour in the soy sauce and cover with a lid (use tin foil if you don't have a lid large enough for your wok). Cook for 3–4 minutes until the cockle shells start to open. Give them a quick stir and then add the pak choi and Chinese broccoli and toss about in the wok for 1–2 minutes until cooked.
. . . . .

Drizzle over the sesame oil, stir in the coriander, divide between four bowls and serve immediately.

A posh version of prawn cocktail. Posh because of the langoustines. Buy them alive and cook them yourself or go for cooked, peeled ones from a fishmonger – the bigger and plumper they are, the better their taste and texture.

Langoustine cocktail with Marie Rose sauce

SERVES 4

100g brown bread,
    cut into cubes
Olive oil, for baking
    the croutons
1 small iceberg lettuce
1–2 lemons, enough for
    10 segments (see method)
2 celery sticks, tough strings
    removed, thinly sliced
2 tablespoons finely
    chopped chives
16 large, fat langoustines,
    cooked and peeled
½ teaspoon smoked paprika
Salt and freshly ground
    white pepper

For the Marie Rose sauce
100g mayonnaise
50g tomato ketchup
Squeeze of lemon juice
1 teaspoon brandy
3 splashes of
    Worcestershire sauce
2 splashes of Tabasco sauce
Pinch of cayenne pepper

First make the Marie Rose sauce by mixing all of the ingredients together in a large bowl. Season to taste with salt and white pepper, put into a clean container and refrigerate until needed.
·····
Preheat the oven to 180°C/Gas Mark 4.
·····
Put the brown bread cubes on a baking tray, trickle over a little olive oil and toss to coat. Bake until crisp, about 8–10 minutes. Remove from the oven and season while still warm with salt and white pepper.
·····
Take the outer leaves from the iceberg lettuce and line four individual serving bowls with them. Thinly slice the remaining iceberg lettuce and put it into a large mixing bowl.
·····
Trim the ends from the lemon and stand it upright on a chopping board. With a small, sharp knife work your way around the fruit, cutting away the peel and outer membrane. Cut the fleshy segments from the inner membrane then lay them out on a roasting tray and give them a blast with a blowtorch until they are charred and blackened. Lift them from the tray and add them to the sliced lettuce.
·····
Add the croutons, celery and chives to the lettuce. Put a couple of tablespoons of the Marie Rose sauce in the bowl and mix together. Season to taste. Divide the mixture between serving bowls and place 4 langoustines on top of each. Trickle on a little more sauce, dust with smoked paprika and serve.

These guys are a bit of work but are so worth it as they're really tasty and make a perfect starter or canapé. You could also use ham in place of the crab. The saffron mayonnaise is easy to make and if you have any left over it will keep sealed in the fridge for a couple of days.

Crab fritters with saffron mayonnaise

MAKES ABOUT 16
BALLS, TO SERVE 4

110ml water
75g butter
110g plain flour, plus
    more for dusting
3 eggs
100g Gruyère cheese, grated
2 tablespoons brown crabmeat
200g white crabmeat,
    well picked over
Finely grated zest of 1 lemon
2 tablespoons chopped chives
1 tablespoon chopped capers
Vegetable oil, for deep-frying
Salt

For the saffron mayonnaise
2 tablespoons olive oil
2 garlic cloves, grated
Generous pinch of
    saffron threads
2 tablespoons pastis
    (anise-flavoured liqueur)
2 tablespoons water
2 egg yolks
2 tablespoons Dijon mustard
2 tablespoons white
    wine vinegar
300ml vegetable oil
Lemon juice, to taste
Cayenne pepper, to taste

First make the saffron mayonnaise. Warm the olive oil in a small pan over a low heat. Add the garlic and saffron. Cook very gently for 1–2 minutes then add the pastis and water and let the saffron steep in the liquid for 5 minutes. Remove from the heat and cool.
.....

Place the egg yolks in a food processor with the mustard and vinegar. Add the infused saffron water and blend together. With the motor running, add the vegetable oil very slowly until it thickens and emulsifies. Season with lemon juice, salt and cayenne pepper, to taste. Transfer to a clean bowl and cover with cling film. Refrigerate until needed.
.....

To make the crab fritters, pour the water into a medium-sized saucepan with the butter and heat until the butter melts. Remove from the heat and add the flour. Mix well until fully incorporated. Beat in the eggs one at a time, using a wooden spoon. Alternatively, you can transfer the dough to a stand mixer. Beat on a slow speed to combine the ingredients, then increase it to medium and beat until smooth and cooled a little.
.....

Beat in the Gruyère and brown crabmeat. Fold in the white crabmeat, lemon zest, chives, capers and a pinch of salt. Leave to go cold. When cold, with lightly floured hands, roll the mixture into walnut-sized balls and place on a lightly floured tray – you should have about 16.
.....

Heat the oil in a deep fat fryer or saucepan to 180°C and lower the balls in gently. Be careful not to crowd the pan – you may need to fry them in batches. Make sure you let the oil come back up to temperature before adding a new batch. Cook until golden brown, about 3–4 minutes. Remove from the fryer, drain on kitchen paper and season with salt and cayenne pepper. Serve immediately with the saffron mayonnaise.

These individual quiches are a little unusual and have a wonderful taste of the sea. The pastry is made with dried seaweed and has a savoury, salty flavour that works really well with the fish. The use of edible seaweed is growing and it is now more widely available in both its fresh and dried forms. If you find it hard to source seaweed where you live, many online suppliers now stock it.

Seafood tarts with seaweed salad

150ml double cream
2 eggs
Few grinds of nutmeg,
    to taste
300g cooked, mixed shellfish
    (mussels, cockles, clams),
    shells removed
75g fresh salmon fillet,
    skinned and diced
70g mixed edible seaweeds
3 tablespoons rice
    wine vinegar
3 tablespoons olive oil
Salt and freshly ground
    white pepper

For the seaweed pastry
250g plain flour, plus
    more for dusting
40g nori seaweed powder
1 teaspoon icing sugar
160g chilled butter, cubed
1 egg yolk
4 tablespoons iced water

First make the pastry by mixing together the flour, seaweed powder, sugar and a pinch of salt in a bowl. Rub in the butter with your fingertips until it forms coarse crumbs. Add the egg yolk and iced water and bring together to form a dough. Remove the dough from the bowl, wrap in cling film and chill for at least 1 hour, or overnight.

. . . . .

Preheat the oven to 170°C/Gas Mark 3. Roll out the pastry on a lightly floured surface until it is as thick as a 20p piece. Cut the pastry into six pieces and use it to line six 10cm loose-bottomed tartlet tins, letting the excess pastry hang over the sides.

. . . . .

Line each tart with some cling film or baking parchment and fill it with baking beans, uncooked pulses or rice. Place the tarts on a baking sheet and bake for 25 minutes until they are cooked and crisp. Take out the cling film and beans and leave the tarts to cool on a rack. With a small, sharp knife, trim off the excess pastry then carefully remove the tarts from the tins. Lower the oven to 150°C/Gas Mark 2.

. . . . .

Whisk together the cream and eggs, season with the nutmeg and a pinch of salt and pepper and pass through a fine sieve. Leave to rest for 20 minutes. Skim any air bubbles from the surface.

. . . . .

Mix together the shellfish and salmon and divide it equally between the tart shells; this will fill them right up. Place the tarts on a baking sheet and gently pour in the seasoned cream and egg. You may not need it all. Bake for 10–15 minutes, until the custards are just set. Remove from the oven and cool for 5–10 minutes before serving.

. . . . .

Meanwhile, mix together the seaweeds, rice wine vinegar and olive oil in a bowl. Dress the top of the tarts with the seaweed and serve.

A simple but delicious way of serving duck. The dish takes a bit of time to prepare but the end result is fantastic. The kebabs are great for a barbecue or served with rice and stir-fried vegetables as a main course.

Duck & lemongrass kebabs

SERVES 4

2 duck breasts, skin on
2 large field mushrooms
2 red onions, peeled
1 green pepper, cored
8 lemongrass sticks
1 large head of broccoli,
    broken into small florets

For the marinade
75ml vegetable oil
75ml dark soy sauce
2 tablespoons runny honey
Juice of 2 limes
3 garlic cloves, grated
3cm piece of fresh ginger,
    peeled and grated
1 red chilli, finely chopped –
    seeds and all

First score the duck breast skin. Using a sharp knife, cut lines into the skin, being careful not to press so hard that you cut into the meat. Try to cut the lines about 5mm apart on a slight angle, then cut them in the opposite direction to form a diamond pattern.
.....
Warm a non-stick frying pan over a medium heat and place the duck breasts in the pan, skin-side down. Let the fat from the breast slowly render (run out into the pan) and cook until the skin is a nice golden brown. When the skin is crisp, remove the breasts and drain them on kitchen paper. Pour the fat away and wipe out the pan. Place the duck breasts in the fridge to chill (this will make it easier to cut the meat later).
.....
Next, make the marinade. Whisk together the oil, soy sauce and honey. Add the lime juice, garlic, ginger and chilli and mix well.
.....
When the duck breasts are chilled, cut them in half lengthways and cut each half into 6–8 even-sized pieces. Cut the mushrooms, onions and pepper into chunks the same size as the duck cubes.
.....
Pierce each duck breast cube and chunk of vegetable with a skewer then thread them on to the lemongrass sticks – these will act as skewers for cooking. Try not to put the same ingredients next to each other. For example, go duck, mushroom, pepper, onion and broccoli, then repeat until the lemongrass stick is full.
.....
When all 8 sticks have been filled, place them in a plastic or glass container and pour over the marinade. Cover and leave for at least 2 hours, or overnight.
.....
Continues overleaf

Duck & lemongrass kebabs

Continued

Remove the kebabs from the fridge at least 30 minutes before you want to cook them. Heat up your barbecue or griddle pan until it's very hot. Barbecue coals should be glowing red and have a fine coating of white ash over the top.

.....

Remove the kebabs from the marinade (reserve the marinade) and pat them dry on kitchen paper. Place them on the barbecue or in the pan and cook, basting with the marinade by brushing it on every 3–4 minutes. Turn the kebabs once or twice so they cook evenly. They will take about 8–10 minutes to cook.

.....

Remove them from the heat and leave to rest for 4–5 minutes before serving.

This is the ultimate finger food. The crispy quail with the hot spice of the pickled chillies and the cool, peppery kohlrabi is a great combination. You do have to think ahead though. The chillies need to be prepared about a month in advance of when you want to serve them – once opened, they keep for a couple of weeks in the fridge and are definitely worth the wait. You'll need some jam jars or Kilner-type jars for preserving them.

Crispy quail with kohlrabi slaw & pickled chillies

SERVES 4 –
2 QUAILS EACH

40g salt
40g runny honey
130ml boiling water
700ml buttermilk
8 quails, spatchcocked then
    cut in half (you can ask your
    butcher to do this for you)
300g plain flour
1 tablespoon salt
1 tablespoon smoked paprika
2 teaspoons cracked
    black pepper
2 teaspoons cayenne pepper
2 teaspoons ground cumin
Vegetable oil, for frying
Flaky sea salt, to finish

For the pickled chillies
900ml water
170g salt
500g large green chillies
2 star anise
½ teaspoon Szechuan
    peppercorns
300ml white wine vinegar
15g caster sugar

First pickle the chillies. Put 600ml of the water and 150g of the salt into a large saucepan and bring to the boil, stirring to dissolve the salt. When the salt has dissolved, remove from the heat and cool. Place the chillies in a bowl or plastic container and pour over the cooled brine. Put a small plate on top to ensure that the chillies are completely submerged. Cover and leave overnight.

. . . . .

The next day, tie the star anise and Szechuan peppercorns up in a small bundle of muslin with kitchen string. Place in a saucepan with 300ml of water, the white wine vinegar, sugar and the remaining 20g of salt and bring to the boil, stirring to dissolve the sugar and salt. Remove from the heat and cool.

. . . . .

Put your jars and their lids in a large pan of water and bring to the boil. Boil them for 5–10 minutes to sterilise them then leave them on a clean tea towel or drying rack to cool and dry thoroughly.

. . . . .

Drain the chillies from the brine and, with a small, sterilised pin, pierce the top of each chilli 4–5 times before putting into the sterilised jars. Pour the boiled, cooled pickle liquor on top. Seal and store in the fridge for 4–5 weeks before using.

. . . . .

To prepare the quail, put the salt and honey in a large bowl, pour on the boiling water and mix until the salt has dissolved. Add the buttermilk and mix thoroughly. Lower the halved quails into the buttermilk brine and leave at room temperature for 3 hours.

. . . . .

Continues overleaf

Crispy quail with kohlrabi slaw & pickled chillies
Continued

For the kohlrabi slaw
2 kohlrabi
2 Spanish onions
1 tablespoon flaky sea salt
3 tablespoons mayonnaise
1 tablespoon Dijon mustard
2 teaspoons caraway seeds,
   toasted until fragrant
   in a dry frying pan
Freshly ground white pepper

To make the slaw, thinly slice the kohlrabi and the onions with a very sharp knife or a mandolin and place them in a bowl. Sprinkle on the flaky sea salt and stir. Leave to one side for 30 minutes so the salt starts to break down the vegetables.
.....

After 30 minutes, tip them into a colander and wash off the salt under cold, running water. Squeeze dry in a clean tea towel or kitchen paper. Mix together the mayonnaise, mustard and caraway seeds and use it to dress the onion and kohlrabi, stirring until well coated; season. Cover and refrigerate until needed.
.....

To make the seasoned flour for the quail, mix together the flour, salt, paprika, black pepper, cayenne pepper and cumin. Remove the quail halves from the buttermilk and pat dry with kitchen paper. Dust them in the flour, shaking off any excess.
.....

Warm a thin layer of vegetable oil in a large, non-stick frying pan over a medium heat and shallow-fry the quail. When they are crisp and golden on one side, flip them over and cook the other side; they will need about 3–4 minutes per side. When browned all over, remove and drain on kitchen paper. You will probably need to do this in batches, so keep the cooked ones warm in a low oven (100°C/Gas Mark ¼) while you make the rest.
.....

Season with flaky sea salt and serve with the kohlrabi slaw and the pickled chillies.

This dish is a nod to the food of that region where northern France meets Germany, Alsace, and its love of porky charcuterie and cabbage. A great starter, the balls also work well as a side dish for roast pork or chicken.

Cabbage balls stuffed with pancetta & cabbage

MAKES 12 BALLS,
TO SERVE 6

2 savoy cabbages
4 tablespoons vegetable oil
100g pancetta, diced
1 onion, diced
250g garlic sausage, diced
50g caster sugar
2 tablespoons caraway seeds
200ml white wine
100ml white wine vinegar
150g sausage meat
3 garlic cloves, grated
200g pig's caul, washed
100g butter
500ml chicken stock
Salt and freshly ground
    black pepper

Peel the outer green leaves from the cabbages – you will need to remove 4–5 layers. Keep these leaves; you will need them later. Quarter the cabbages, remove the core and slice them finely.
.....

Warm the vegetable oil in a large saucepan over a medium heat and fry the pancetta until its fat renders (runs out into the pan). Stir in the onion and cook for 2–3 minutes. Add the garlic sausage, caster sugar and caraway seeds, stir and add the wine and vinegar. Tip in the sliced cabbage. Bring to the boil, stir and simmer until the liquid has evaporated, being careful not to let the mixture catch on the bottom. Remove from the heat, cool at room temperature, then chill in the fridge.
.....

Cut the tough middle stalks from the reserved outer cabbage leaves, then cut the leaves in half. Bring a pan of salted water to the boil and have a bowl of iced water ready next to the hob. Put the leaves into the boiling water and cook until just softened – this will take 2–3 minutes. Quickly drain the cabbage leaves and refresh in the iced water to stop them cooking. Drain again and dry on a clean tea towel.
.....

In a large mixing bowl, combine the chilled cabbage mixture with the sausage meat and garlic; season. Separate the mixture into 12 equal-sized balls. Wrap these balls in the blanched cabbage leaves and then wrap each one in a double layer of the pig's caul – this will hold them together when you cook them later. Pop the cabbage balls on to a plate and stick them in the fridge for 1 hour.
.....

Preheat the oven to 180°C/Gas Mark 4. Put the cabbage balls in a roasting tin in which they fit snugly and place a little butter on top of each one. Pour in the stock and cook for 20–25 minutes, basting at least 3 times during the cooking, until they are hot in the middle. Pour the cooking liquid into a saucepan and keep the tin of cabbage balls warm in a low oven (100°C/Gas Mark ¼). Simmer the liquid until it has reduced and thickened into a glaze. Pour over the cabbage balls and serve immediately.

These ribs are the perfect accompaniment to a pint. They take about an hour to cook and taste great, even better if you can manage to marinate them overnight. Tamarind, sometimes called 'the Indian date', has a slightly sour flavour and is a key ingredient in Worcestershire sauce.

Baby back ribs with ale & tamarind

SERVES 4

6 tablespoons tamarind paste
6 garlic cloves, grated
2 tablespoons dark
   muscovado sugar
2 teaspoons ground turmeric
2 teaspoons chilli powder
2 teaspoons yellow
   mustard seeds
2 teaspoons cracked
   black pepper
2 teaspoons salt
290ml dark ale, porter or stout
2 racks of baby back pork
   ribs, trimmed and cleaned
   of all sinew

To serve
1 iceberg lettuce, finely sliced
Bunch of coriander,
   chopped – stalks and all
Juice of 1 lemon
Drizzle of rapeseed oil

In a large mixing bowl, whisk together the tamarind paste, garlic, sugar, turmeric, chilli powder, mustard seeds, pepper and salt. Pour in the dark ale and mix thoroughly. Place the trimmed racks in a large, shallow bowl or roasting tin and pour on the marinade. Roll the ribs around in the marinade, making sure that they get completely covered. Cover with cling film and place in the fridge for at least 2 hours, but overnight is better.

. . . . .

Preheat the oven to 180°C/Gas Mark 4.

. . . . .

Lift the ribs out of their marinade. Reserve the marinade because you will use it to baste the ribs as they cook. Place an ovenproof cake or cooling rack over a roasting tin and put the ribs on top. This will allow the hot air to circulate and fat to drip down.

. . . . .

Pop the tray into the oven and roast for 15 minutes. Turn the ribs over and baste them with the remaining marinade. Repeat this process 2 or 3 more times – the ribs will take about 45–60 minutes to cook. When cooked, the meat will begin to ease back from the ends of the bones. Take the ribs out of the oven and leave to rest for 5–10 minutes before serving.

. . . . .

While the meat is resting, place the iceberg lettuce in a bowl with the chopped coriander. Season and mix with the lemon juice and rapeseed oil. Serve with the ribs.

This toastie is a play on Welsh rarebit and an adaptation of what I think is the best ever recipe for it, created by the great Gary Rhodes. The recipe does make more topping mixture than you need, but it freezes brilliantly – and I reckon that after you've tried a toastie, you'll be craving another – as an easy supper or when those late-night, post-pub munchies attack!

Ham & cheese toastie

MAKES 6

700g best-quality
    Cheddar cheese
150ml milk
50g fresh breadcrumbs
30g plain flour
1 tablespoon English
    mustard powder
Cayenne pepper, to taste
Good splash of
    Worcestershire sauce
2 eggs
2 egg yolks
300g ham, diced
6 thick slices of white bread
Salt

Put the Cheddar into a saucepan with the milk and heat gently, stirring with a wooden spoon, to melt the cheese. When it's melted, stir in the breadcrumbs, flour and mustard powder and cook for a few minutes, stirring. Season with salt, cayenne pepper and Worcestershire sauce. Remove from the heat, tip into a food processor and blend. Add the eggs and egg yolks and blend again until smooth. Scrape the mixture into a bowl, fold in the diced ham and mix thoroughly – it will be a very thick paste.

. . . . .

Toast the bread on both sides, then spread it with a layer of the ham and cheese mixture so that the toasted bread is completely covered. Place under a hot grill and cook until the mixture is bubbling and golden brown. Serve straight away. And then come back and toast some more for seconds. You know you want to.

. . . . .

To freeze the leftover mixture, place it on a large piece of baking parchment, cover with a second piece of baking parchment and roll out to the thickness of a £1 coin. Place on a baking sheet and freeze. When frozen, wrap in cling film then return to the freezer until needed. You may want to cut it into portions that fit more easily in your freezer. To cook from frozen, simply cut a piece of mixture to fit your bread and cook as above.

This tasty 'butter' is delicious simply spread on toast, but it's also great as a sauce for pasta or just stuck on top of a baked potato. If you're not serving this number of people, it will keep well in the fridge for a week or you can freeze it for up to 3 months.

Ham butter with hot toast

SERVES 8-10

1 smoked ham hock,
    about 1.2kg
1 tablespoon black
    peppercorns
1 tablespoon coriander seeds
1 tablespoon fennel seeds
1 onion, quartered
1 whole garlic bulb,
    halved horizontally
2 carrots
2 celery sticks
Vegetable oil, for frying
250g butter, at room
    temperature
2 banana shallots,
    very finely diced
2 egg yolks
4 tablespoons prepared
    English mustard
2 tablespoons white
    wine vinegar
2 tablespoons yellow
    mustard seeds, lightly
    toasted in a dry frying pan
2 tablespoons finely
    chopped flat-leaf parsley
1 tablespoon finely
    chopped chervil
1 teaspoon curry powder
1 teaspoon cayenne pepper
8-10 thick slices of
    sourdough bread
Salt and freshly ground
    black pepper

Place the ham hock in a large saucepan and cover with cold water. Place on the hob and bring to the boil, then drain and cover with fresh water. Tie the peppercorns, coriander seeds and fennel seeds together in a muslin bag and place the bag in the pan. Add the onion, garlic, carrots and celery and bring to the boil. Turn the heat down to a simmer and cook gently for 2½ hours until the ham hock is cooked – keep an eye on it and if the liquid looks a little low, add a splash of boiling water from the kettle. Leave to cool in the stock.

When the ham hock is cool, pick the ham from the bone and remove any sinew and skin (don't discard the stock; keep it for making pea and ham soup). Flake and finely shred the meat. Warm a little oil in a frying pan over a medium–high heat and fry the ham until crisp. Drain on some kitchen paper and leave to cool.

In a stand mixer with a beater attachment, slowly soften the butter. Add the shallots, egg yolks, mustard, vinegar, mustard seeds, parsley, chervil, curry powder and cayenne pepper. When it's all smooth and bound together, add the crispy ham. Season.

Transfer the butter to a small terrine or serving dish, then put in the fridge for at least 1 hour before you serve it.

Let the butter come to room temperature, toast the sourdough then spread the softened butter on top. Serve immediately.

A mix of all things ace! The ham fritters go so well with the creamy, rich cheese fondue; the addition of the onion chutney gives a sweet balance and then you get the acidic bitter crunch of the chicory. Lush.

Ham fritters with cheese fondue

SERVES 6

250g plain flour, plus
    a bit more for dusting
20g fresh yeast, crumbled
500ml milk
Vegetable oil, for deep-frying
500–600g whole piece
    of cooked ham, cut into
    bite-sized chunks
Salt and freshly ground
    black pepper

For the fondue
2 large onions, skin on
300ml white wine
300g Gruyère cheese, grated
150g Epoisses cheese, chopped
150g Comté cheese, grated
2 teaspoons cornflour mixed
    with 3 tablespoons water
Few grinds of nutmeg
Freshly ground white pepper

For the chutney
3 tablespoons cider vinegar
1½ tablespoons dark
    muscovado sugar
1 small Bramley apple, grated
1 tablespoon yellow
    mustard seeds

Preheat the oven to 160°C/Gas Mark 3.

· · · · ·

The first job is to slow-roast the onions for the fondue. Place the onions on a baking tray and roast in the oven for about 2½ hours until semi-soft. Remove from the oven and leave to cool.

· · · · ·

When cold, gently cut the fuzzy root off, about a third of the way down each onion. Gently scoop the middle out, leaving about 3 layers to form a hollow onion. You are going to serve the fondue inside the onions, so be careful to keep them intact. Place the onion shells to one side until needed and chop up the scooped-out onion middles quite roughly.

· · · · ·

Next, make the chutney. Put the vinegar into a non-stick saucepan with the sugar. Warm over a high heat, stirring to dissolve the sugar, and bring to the boil. Add the chopped onion middles, Bramley apple and mustard seeds. Turn the heat down and cook, stirring from time to time, until you have a tasty chutney – this won't take too long, about 20–25 minutes. Remove from the heat and leave to cool. When cold, you can put it in a container and chill until needed. It will keep for a week in the fridge and is lush with a big piece of Cheddar!

· · · · ·

To make the batter for the fritters, put the flour into a mixing bowl with the yeast and make a well in the middle. Gently warm the milk to body temperature (if you put a clean finger in it, it should feel neither hot nor cold) and whisk it into the flour mixture. Leave to one side for 1 hour while the yeast starts to work and ferment.

· · · · ·

Continues overleaf

Ham fritters with cheese fondue
Continued

For the pickled chicory
500ml Pickle liquor
(see p. 291)
6 chicory heads,
leaves separated

To serve
Radishes, with their
leaves on
Simple Treviso or
other bitter-leaf
salad (optional)

To make the fondue, bring the white wine to the boil in a saucepan. Turn the heat right down to a simmer and add the cheeses, stirring to melt them gently. Add the cornflour mixture and cook for 5 minutes, stirring frequently on a low heat, until the cheese is completely melted and the fondue has thickened. Season with the nutmeg, pepper and a pinch of salt if needed. Keep warm over a very gentle heat while you fry the fritters.

. . . . .

When the fritter batter is ready, heat the vegetable oil in a deep fat fryer to 180°C. Dust the chunks of ham with a little flour, dip them into the batter a few at a time and then gently lower them into the hot oil. Cook for 4–5 minutes until golden and crisp. You may need to do this in batches, so make sure you let the fat come back up to temperature before adding more fritters. Drain on kitchen paper and season.

. . . . .

To pickle the chicory, pour the pickle liquor into a non-metallic bowl then stick the chicory leaves into the bowl for a few seconds.

. . . . .

Pour the fondue into the hollow onions and serve with the ham fritters and onion chutney. On the side, serve the pickled chicory and some radishes with salt, or a bitter-leaf salad. Dip the crispy fritters into the fondue and dab on a little chutney. OMG...

This is based on a classic pork farmhouse terrine but the lamb makes a nice change. It is very rich and full of flavour, with gentle spicing, and the fragrant coriander salad is its perfect match. If you don't own a coarse meat grinder, you can ask your butcher to grind the meats for you, though the flavour and texture of the terrine will be slightly different. It will keep for 5–6 days in the fridge.

Spiced lamb terrine with flatbreads

MAKES A 1.4KG TERRINE, ENOUGH TO SERVE 10–15 PEOPLE

3 dried bay leaves
1 tablespoon coriander seeds
1 teaspoon cumin seeds
1 teaspoon yellow
    mustard seeds
1 teaspoon pink peppercorns
1 teaspoon whole
    black peppercorns
900g trimmed, lean
    boneless lamb shank,
    cut into 2cm cubes
450g lamb breast, diced
450g pork belly, diced
180ml double cream
15g fresh breadcrumbs
4 teaspoons salt
1 teaspoon saltpetre
    (available online, optional)
200g pig's caul, washed

Preheat the oven to 180°C/Gas Mark 4.

.....

Put the bay leaves, coriander seeds, cumin seeds, mustard seeds and both types of peppercorn on a baking tray and bake for 4–5 minutes until toasted. Remove from the oven and tip on to a plate to cool. When cold, blend in a spice grinder or with a pestle and mortar.

.....

Put the lamb shank, lamb breast and pork belly into a large bowl with the ground spices. Mix well and cover with cling film. Place in the fridge overnight.

.....

The next day, mince the spiced meat with a coarse grinder and place in a large bowl.

.....

In a saucepan, gently warm the double cream to body temperature (if you put a finger in it, it should feel neither hot nor cold) and mix in the breadcrumbs. Stir until the cream thickens. Remove from the heat and leave to cool.

.....

Preheat the oven to 150°C/Gas Mark 2.

.....

Add the salt and saltpetre, if using, to the mince, then pour in the thickened double cream and mix together with your hands until you feel the mix become a little 'tighter' and it begins to form a ball. Line a 1.4kg terrine mould with a double layer of the pig's caul, leaving some excess hanging over the sides. Push in the lamb mix, making sure you get it right into the corners of the mould. Fill the terrine right to the brim and then wrap the excess pig's caul over the top of the meat. Put the lid on or cover very tightly with foil.

.....

Continues overleaf

Spiced lamb terrine with flatbreads
Continued

For the flatbreads
250g strong white flour,
  plus more for kneading
  and rolling
½ teaspoon salt
4 tablespoons olive oil
100ml warm water

For the salad
½ iceberg lettuce, shredded
1 bunch of coriander, leaves
  torn from the stems and
  stems finely chopped
½ teaspoon coriander seeds,
  toasted in a dry frying
  pan and crushed
Juice of ½ lemon
75ml extra virgin olive oil
Salt and freshly ground
  black pepper

Place a J-cloth in the bottom of a roasting tin and put the terrine on top. Pour about 5–8cm of boiling water into the tin and carefully place it in the oven. Cook for an hour, or until the middle of the terrine reaches 65°C on a digital temperature probe. When it has come to temperature, remove from the oven, take the mould out of the roasting tin and leave to cool at room temperature. Once cool, place it in the fridge overnight to chill thoroughly.

· · · · ·

To make the flatbreads, mix the flour and the salt together in a bowl and make a well in the centre. Add the olive oil and then slowly add the warm water, stirring and bringing the paste together to make a dough. Knead into a tight ball and leave to rest, covered with cling film, for 30 minutes.

· · · · ·

After the dough has rested, divide it into 6 equal balls. On a surface lightly dusted with flour, roll each portion into an oval shape about 5mm thick. Heat a non-stick frying pan over a medium heat. Add as many flatbreads as will fit and dry fry for 2–3 minutes on each side until lightly toasted and crisp. You may need to do this in batches.

· · · · ·

Put the iceberg lettuce in a mixing bowl with the coriander leaves and chopped stems. Sprinkle with the crushed coriander seeds. Add the lemon juice and the olive oil and season. Toss together.

· · · · ·

To turn out the terrine, sit it in some hot water for a minute and it should release from the base and sides. Slice and serve with the flatbreads and salad.

salads
& soups

However ambitious I am about food and how adventurous it can be, I know that on a menu it can be reassuring to have some key familiar dishes – a soup, a terrine, a steak. Seeing these things makes people feel comfortable, confident that they're going to have a good time.

And then you can bring in the surprises. Yes, I'll give you a lovely bowl of celery soup, but then I'll poach an egg and roll it in the chopped celery leaves before floating it in the bowl. Or I'll increase the flavour in some gorgeous roasted red pepper soup by spooning in some punchy red onion and anchovy salsa.

I've always loved soup – making it, thinking about it, eating it. When I first started working in kitchens, often the soups were pretty miserable things – just the blended version of yesterday's leftover vegetables. I certainly didn't want to do that in my own restaurant; I was keen to handle a soup's ingredients with as much care as I did the rest of the menu.

One of my favourite recipes in this book is the Garlic and brown bread soup because it takes simple, homely ingredients and elevates them to a new level. I roast the onions and garlic with lemon for several hours then serve them with a beautiful, lemony burnt butter – it's about as far away from blitzed-up leftovers as you can get.

The principle is the same with salads. When you're serving just a few things on a plate, there's nowhere for the less-than-brilliant produce to hide, so you want the ingredients to be the very best you can find and you need to treat them carefully.

Salads are about balance, with maybe the odd surprise thrown in. That's why I'm so fond of the Crispy duck salad – lovely shredded meat; juicy, sweet watermelon and pomegranate; a bit of heat from the chilli; and a whack of freshness from the coriander and mint. And it looks beautiful too. Who could ask for more than that?

Coleslaw is one of my favourite garnishes or salads. You can use such a wide variety of vegetables and they all give a different layer of taste and texture. Have a good play around to find your own favourites but this is my preferred mix. Folding in a flavoured mayonnaise lifts it to new heights. I use garlic here, but a lemon-mayonnaise coleslaw will go well with fish, and a herby one is delicious alongside roast chicken.

Hard-core coleslaw

SERVES 6-8

1 fennel bulb
¼ small red cabbage
¼ small white cabbage
¼ small celeriac, peeled
2 large carrots, peeled
1 raw beetroot, peeled
1 Spanish onion
2 tablespoons flaky sea salt
Finely grated zest of 1 lemon
1 tablespoon fennel seeds,
    lightly toasted in a dry
    frying pan
1 teaspoon chopped dill
1 tablespoon chopped chervil
1 tablespoon chopped
    flat-leaf parsley

For the dressing
2 egg yolks
35g prepared English mustard
20ml white wine vinegar
2 teaspoons caster sugar
Juice of 1 lemon
5 garlic cloves, grated
1 tablespoon chopped
    salted anchovies
350ml vegetable oil
Cayenne pepper, to taste
Salt

First remove the tough core from the fennel and cabbages. Shred them finely either with a sharp knife or with a mandolin, along with the celeriac, carrots, beetroot and onion. Place them all in a large mixing bowl. Add the flaky sea salt and mix thoroughly. Leave to soften for 20 minutes.
.....
Meanwhile, make the dressing. Place the egg yolks, mustard, vinegar, sugar, lemon juice, garlic and anchovies in a food processor and blend until smooth. With the motor running, slowly pour in the oil through the feed tube until the mayonnaise is smooth and emulsified. Season to taste with salt and cayenne pepper then pass the mayonnaise through a fine sieve to make it really smooth. This can be made ahead of time and stored, sealed, in the fridge for up to a week.
.....
Place the vegetables in a colander and rinse under cold, running water for 2–3 minutes, then leave to drain. Place them in a clean tea towel and squeeze out the excess moisture. Put them into a clean mixing bowl. Add the lemon zest, fennel seeds and herbs and check the seasoning. Fold in enough mayonnaise to coat generously. You may not need it all. Mix together well and serve.

This is a bit of an old-school recipe, a 1970s throwback that stands the taste test of time. Served cold, the mushrooms make a great salad dish for barbecues and summer Sunday lunches in the garden. Mushrooms have so much body to them, they're both filling and work like little sponges to absorb loads of flavour.

Mushrooms à la Grecque

SERVES 4

250ml white wine
100ml extra virgin olive oil
1 onion, finely diced
2 bay leaves
2 garlic cloves, grated
1 tablespoon coriander seeds
1 tablespoon demerara sugar
Juice and grated zest of
   1 lemon
500g button mushrooms,
   washed and stalks removed
Salt and freshly ground
   black pepper

Place all the ingredients apart from the mushrooms in a saucepan and bring to the boil. Put the mushrooms in a bowl or pan, pour the hot liquid over the top and cover with cling film to keep the heat in, then let the mushrooms sit and gently take on the flavours.

.....

When cool, season and place in a cold, sterilised Kilner-type jar and store in the fridge until needed. The mushrooms will keep for up to 2 weeks. Simple.

Buying raw beetroot from a farmers' market or shop rather than using pre-cooked beetroot will make a big difference to the flavour of this salad – the true earthiness of the vegetable shines through. It goes very well with game and oily fish.

Beetroot with celery leaves & redcurrant glaze

4 large raw beetroots, trimmed but unpeeled
150ml red wine vinegar
2 tablespoons redcurrant jelly
2 cloves
75g Dijon mustard
5 tablespoons roughly chopped celery leaves
4 tablespoons pine nuts, lightly toasted in a dry frying pan
1 bunch of chives, finely chopped

For the crème fraîche
100g crème fraîche
½ teaspoon smoked paprika
½ teaspoon salt
¼ teaspoon cayenne pepper
Finely grated zest of 1 lemon

To garnish
4 celery sticks, tough strings removed
Flaky sea salt
Juice of ½ lemon
Rapeseed oil, for drizzling
2 tablespoons finely chopped parsley

Place the beetroots in a large saucepan and cover with water. Bring to the boil, turn the heat down to a simmer and add a good pinch of salt. Cook the beetroots for about 1 hour, or until they are tender when pierced with a small, sharp knife. Drain in a colander and leave the beetroots to steam dry. While they are still warm, remove the skins by peeling them off with your hands – they should just rub off. Trim off the root and leave to cool.
.....

Put the vinegar, redcurrant jelly and cloves into a small saucepan, bring to the boil and bubble to reduce to a thickened glaze. Remove from the heat, take out the cloves then whisk in the mustard.
.....

Cut the cooked beetroot into large chunks and place in a mixing bowl. Pour on the redcurrant mixture and fold it all in together. Stir in the celery leaves, pine nuts and chives.
.....

Whisk together the crème fraîche, smoked paprika, salt, cayenne pepper and lemon zest until it's nice and thick.
.....

To finish, use a sharp vegetable peeler to peel the celery sticks into long, thin strips and place in a mixing bowl. Season with a pinch of flaky sea salt and lemon juice, drizzle over some rapeseed oil and mix in the parsley.
.....

Divide the beetroot between serving plates. Place some celery mixture on top along with a dollop of crème fraîche and serve.

This is a great salad, perfect to serve with spring lamb. The salty feta makes a big impact and the mildly flavoured courgettes are a great foil for the rest of the contrasting flavours. Serve it with a slow-roast leg or shoulder of lamb or simply on toast for a light lunch or supper.

Courgette & feta salad

SERVES 4

100g feta cheese, crumbled
2 Little Gem lettuces,
    leaves separated
100g pitted black olives,
    roughly chopped
1 green pepper, cored,
    deseeded and finely diced
1 bunch of mint, leaves only
½ bunch of coriander,
    leaves removed, stalks
    finely chopped
½ green chilli, finely sliced
½ red chilli, finely sliced
100g rendered lamb fat or
    leftover lamb dripping
    or 100ml olive oil
4 courgettes, cut diagonally
    into 4–5mm thick slices
25ml sherry vinegar
Salt

Place the feta, lettuce, olives, green pepper, mint leaves, coriander leaves and stalks, and chillies on a large serving platter.
.....
Warm a little lamb fat in a large, non-stick frying pan over a high heat. Add the sliced courgettes in batches, being careful not to crowd the pan, and fry until golden – about a couple of minutes on each side. Once all the batches are cooked, sprinkle with a little salt.
.....
Place the frying pan back on the heat and warm the remaining lamb fat. Add the courgettes to the salad, drizzle over the sherry vinegar and warm lamb fat, and serve immediately.

This is a big-flavoured salad with loads of texture and a smoothness that comes from the nutty mayonnaise. You will need a blowtorch for this, but the great bitter flavour that you get from the charred chicory is incredible, so it's worth the investment if you don't have one already.

Charred chicory & mackerel with nut oil mayonnaise

SERVES 2

2 red chicory, quartered lengthways

2 large mackerel, the freshest you can find, filleted, boned and cut in half (ask your fishmonger to do this for you if you like)

Salt and freshly ground black pepper

For the dressing

75ml extra virgin olive oil, plus more for drizzling

3 tablespoons toasted hazelnuts, crushed a little

2 tablespoons finely chopped chives

2 tablespoons Cabernet Sauvignon vinegar

For the mayonnaise

2 egg yolks

30g Dijon mustard

4 tsp white wine vinegar

Juice of ½ lemon

1 garlic clove, grated

200ml vegetable oil

150ml hazelnut oil

Cayenne pepper, to taste

To make the mayonnaise, place the egg yolks, mustard, vinegar, lemon juice and garlic in a food processor and blend until smooth. With the motor still running, very slowly add the two oils until the mixture thickens and emulsifies into a mayonnaise. If it is very thick, thin slightly with a splash of warm water. Season with salt and cayenne pepper, to taste, then pour into a squeezy bottle and refrigerate until needed. It will keep for up to a week in the fridge.

.....

To make the dressing, mix together the olive oil, hazelnuts, chives and vinegar in a bowl. Season and set aside.

.....

Place the chicory on a metal tray, drizzle with olive oil and blowtorch them until they take on a charred colour and flavour. Spoon on a little of the hazelnut dressing.

.....

Put the mackerel fillets on to the tray and drizzle with a little more olive oil. Blowtorch one side to give them a charred colour, then flip over and repeat on the other side. Don't overcook them – you want them to be raw in the middle.

.....

Spread a spoonful of mayonnaise on to two serving plates, place the chicory and mackerel on top, then spoon over some more dressing. Serve immediately.

Inspired by a dish I first tasted when I was working with chef Simon Bradley at Odette's restaurant in North London, this salad has a lovely balance of flavours. It's hot, cold, spicy and refreshing all at the same time. A great one for summer!

Crispy duck salad

Preheat the oven to 160°C/Gas Mark 3.
.....

Place an ovenproof wire rack on top of a baking tray and put the duck legs on top. Bake for 1¾–2 hours until the legs are crisp and cooked. Remove from the oven and cool for 10 minutes. Set aside the duck fat (still in the tray) for later.
.....

Place the watermelon in a large mixing bowl. Cut the pomegranate in half and remove the seeds by holding each half over the bowl, turning them upside down and banging the skin side with a fork. The seeds should just drop out.
.....

Add the coriander leaves and stalks, mint, and red chilli to the mix. Pour over the lime juice, Thai fish sauce and soy sauce. Flake in the crispy duck meat and season with the Szechuan pepper. Mix thoroughly and serve while the duck is still warm and the watermelon cold. The temperature contrast and the mix of salt, sweet and sour are fantastic!

SERVES 4

4 large duck legs
½ watermelon, chilled, cut into bite-sized pieces – try to leave some of the black seeds in place
1 pomegranate
1 bunch of coriander, leaves removed and stalks finely chopped
½ bunch of mint, leaves only, roughly torn
1 or 2 long, red chillies, finely sliced – seeds and all
Juice of 2 limes
2 tablespoons Thai fish sauce
2 tablespoons dark soy sauce
½ teaspoon ground Szechuan pepper

Quick and easy to make, this flavoursome soup is perfect for summer lunches. The pesto and the basil oil last for a few days sealed in the fridge – they're also really good for dressing pizzas or simple pasta dishes.

Roasted tomato soup

SERVES 4-6

50g butter
1 onion, finely diced
4 garlic cloves, grated
2 red chillies, finely
    chopped – seeds and all
100g caster sugar
250ml red wine vinegar
2kg ripe plum tomatoes,
    cut into chunks (do not
    peel or deseed)
2 thick slices of white
    bread, roughly torn
1 large bunch of basil
1 teaspoon cayenne pepper
Salt and freshly ground
    black pepper

For the basil oil
1 large bunch of basil,
    leaves only
150ml olive oil

For the pesto
1 large bunch of basil,
    leaves only
50g pine nuts
50g Parmesan cheese, grated
2 garlic cloves, finely grated
150ml olive oil

To make the soup, melt the butter in a large, heavy-bottomed saucepan over a low heat and sweat the onion until it's soft but hasn't taken on any colour – about 15 minutes. Add a pinch of salt to the onion while it's cooking. Add the garlic and chilli and cook for a further 2–3 minutes. Stir in the sugar and vinegar, bring to the boil and simmer until reduced by a quarter. Add the tomatoes, cover with a lid and cook on a medium heat until they have broken down and are soft, about 15 minutes.
.....
Add the bread, then stir in the basil – stalks and leaves – and a little of the cayenne pepper and bring to the boil. Remove from the heat and let the bread soak up some juice to thicken the soup, then leave it for about 15 minutes.
.....
To make the basil oil, bring a saucepan of salted water to the boil and place a small bowl of iced water by the hob. Blanch the basil leaves for 10 seconds, then immediately plunge them into the iced water. Drain and pat dry on kitchen paper. Put the leaves into a blender or food processor, add the olive oil and whizz until smooth. Season to taste. Pass the oil through a muslin cloth or thin tea towel. Set aside.
.....
To make the pesto, put the basil leaves, pine nuts, Parmesan cheese, garlic and a pinch of salt into the blender or food processor. Pulse to a coarse paste, slowly adding the olive oil through the feed tube. Remove and place in a small serving bowl.
.....
Pour the soup into the cleaned blender or food processor and whizz until smooth. Season with salt and more cayenne pepper. Pass the soup through a fine sieve. Gently reheat the soup and pour it into warmed bowls. Trickle on some basil oil. Serve immediately with the pesto alongside.

I love celery. It's a versatile vegetable, with a fragrant flavour that I think of as being very British. Celery makes a great soup on its own but here I serve it with poached eggs to add a bit of depth and richness.

Cream of celery soup with poached eggs

SERVES 4-6

Rapeseed oil, for cooking and dressing
1 onion, diced
2 garlic cloves, grated
1 potato, peeled and diced
1 litre chicken stock
1kg celery head, tough strings removed, thinly sliced; leaves reserved and finely chopped
1 bunch of flat-leaf parsley, leaves only
200ml double cream
White wine vinegar
6 eggs, as fresh as possible so the whites hold their shape
Celery salt
Salt

Warm a splash of rapeseed oil in a large, heavy-bottomed saucepan over a medium heat. Add the onion and garlic and sweat gently until soft, stirring from time to time, about 10–15 minutes. Add the potato and cook for a further 5–6 minutes.

.....

Pour the chicken stock into the pan and bring to the boil. Turn down to a simmer and cook until the potato is soft – about 10–12 minutes. Add the celery to the pan and bring to the boil. Cook for 5–8 minutes, until the celery is just soft.

.....

Stir in the parsley leaves and cook for a further 2–3 minutes. Pour in the double cream, stir, then remove from the heat. Whizz in a blender or food processor until smooth then pass through a fine sieve and season. If you're not eating the soup straight away, pour it into a bowl placed in another bowl filled with ice and water so it cools down as quickly as possible and retains its beautiful green colour.

.....

Place the chopped celery leaf on a plate. Bring a large saucepan of salted water to the boil and stir in a large splash of white wine vinegar. Crack the eggs into the water one by one. Turn the heat down to a gentle simmer and poach the eggs for 3–5 minutes, until the whites are just set. Remove them from the water with a slotted spoon and put them on to kitchen paper. Drizzle the eggs with a little rapeseed oil and then gently roll them in the celery leaf.

.....

Pour the hot soup into warmed serving bowls and place a poached egg in each bowl. Drizzle a little more rapeseed oil over the top and give each one a good sprinkling of celery salt. Serve immediately.

A very British equivalent of gazpacho, this super summer soup is fantastic for serving at a barbecue. If you're feeling a little bit dangerous, it works really well with a good splash of frozen vodka.

Chilled cucumber soup

SERVES 8

3 cucumbers
1–2 tablespoons rapeseed oil
1 onion, diced
200g Greek yoghurt
3–4 large green chillies,
    finely sliced – seeds and all
Juice and finely grated zest
    of 2 limes
1 bunch of chives,
    finely chopped
500ml iced sparkling water
Salt and freshly ground
    white pepper

To serve
Ice cubes
½ bunch of mint,
    small leaves only
Ice-cold vodka (optional)

Peel the cucumbers and split them in half lengthways. Scoop out the seeds and discard. Chop the cucumber flesh into rough 5cm chunks.
.....
Warm the rapeseed oil in a heavy-bottomed saucepan over a medium heat. Add the onion and cook for about 15 minutes, until soft, stirring from time to time. Add the cucumber and a good pinch of salt to help break it down. Cook for about 3–4 minutes then remove from the heat. Leave to cool.
.....
Put the cucumber and onion into a large mixing bowl with the yoghurt, half the chilli, the lime juice and zest, and the chives, then stir. Add the sparkling water to the bowl and stir – the sparkling water helps make this soup really light and airy. Whizz the soup in a blender or food processor until smooth then pass through a fine sieve into a container. Season, cover and place in the fridge until thoroughly chilled – at least a couple of hours. Stir before serving.
.....
Add a couple of ice cubes to each of the serving bowls or glasses and ladle the soup over the top. Sprinkle on the mint and the remaining sliced chilli and dot with a few drops of rapeseed oil, if liked. Serve with a big splash of frozen vodka if you want to live life to the full!

This soup's stock is infused with baked potato skins, which give it real depth of flavour. The broth is light and clean but the potato dumplings make it hearty. You can also add all sorts of extra ingredients such as strips of beef or pieces of cooked chicken to make it more substantial.

Baked potato broth with dumplings

SERVES 4-6

2 red onions, skin on
1 large Spanish onion, skin on
1.2 litres Rich chicken stock
    (see p. 285)
Flaky sea salt
50g butter
200g button or pearl
    onions, peeled
1 bunch of spring onions,
    finely chopped
1 bunch of chives,
    finely chopped
Salt and freshly ground
    black pepper
Chive flowers, to garnish

For the dumplings
2 very large baking potatoes,
    about 800g in total
3 teaspoons garlic powder
2 teaspoons salt
2 teaspoons dried sage
1 teaspoon onion powder
200g plain flour, plus more
    for dusting
1 egg, lightly beaten

Preheat the oven to 180°C/Gas Mark 4.
.....
Start with the dumplings. Bake the potatoes for 1½ hours or until they're soft in the middle and crisp on the outside. Remove from the oven (leave the oven on) and cool for 15 minutes. Cut the potatoes in half, scrape out the middles and put them through a potato ricer. Make sure you keep the skins.
.....
Weigh out 200g of mashed potato and place it in a large bowl – discard the rest. Add the garlic powder, salt, sage and onion powder. Fold in the flour and egg to make a dough. Knead the mixture with your hands and roll into a large ball. Pinch off amounts about the size of large marbles. Dust your hands with a little flour and roll these into balls in the palms of your hands. Put them on a plate lined with cling film, cover and place in the fridge to rest for at least 30 minutes.
.....
Preheat the oven to 180°C/Gas Mark 4. Peel the red and Spanish onions and place the onion skins on a baking tray. Cut the reserved potato skins in half and then place them on the tray too. Bake for 10–15 minutes, until crisp. The kitchen should smell of 'extreme' baked potato. Remove from the oven.
.....
Bring the chicken stock to the boil in a large saucepan and then put the baked potato skins and onion skins into the stock. Remove the pan from the heat and cover with cling film. Leave to infuse like a cup of tea for 20 minutes, to take on the potato and onion flavours. Pass the broth through a fine sieve into a clean saucepan and season.
.....
Continues overleaf

Baked potato broth with dumplings

Continued

Bring a large pan of salted water to the boil, then place the chilled dumplings in the water a few at a time and turn the heat down. You will need to do this in batches so you don't crowd the pan, but make sure you bring the liquid back to the boil between batches. Gently poach the dumplings until they float – that's when you know they are cooked. Carefully lift them from the pan with a slotted spoon and place them on a plate.

.....

Slice the red and Spanish onions very thinly and place them in a colander. Sprinkle with a little flaky sea salt and leave them to break down for 5–10 minutes. Wash under cold, running water and pat dry on kitchen paper. Place the wilted onions in the bottom of your serving bowls.

.....

In a frying pan over a medium heat, melt the butter then add the button onions and fry gently. Add a pinch of salt and continue to fry for 5–8 minutes until they're just cooked and have taken on a little colour. Add the button onions to the bowls with the wilted onions.

.....

Bring the baked potato broth to the boil then add the dumplings to warm them through. Turn the heat down and leave to simmer for 1–2 minutes.

.....

Sprinkle the spring onions and chives into the serving bowls. Ladle the potato broth over the top with some of the dumplings. Tear off some petals from the chive flower heads, sprinkle them over the soup and serve immediately.

A tasty nod to the warmth of Spain, this soup is layered with sweet and salty flavours and it could easily be used as a cooking sauce for fish or white meat. The recipe makes more salsa than you need but any leftovers are delicious spread on a bit of chargrilled bread or toast.

Roast red pepper soup with anchovy salsa

Extra virgin olive oil,
   for cooking
6 red peppers, cored,
   deseeded and cut
   into quarters
2 onions, diced
6 garlic cloves, grated
2 red chillies, stems removed,
   chopped – seeds and all
50g caster sugar
Generous pinch of
   saffron threads
3½ tablespoons pastis
   (anise-flavoured liqueur)
100ml red wine vinegar
500ml chicken or
   vegetable stock
100ml double cream
Cayenne pepper, to taste
Salt and freshly ground
   black pepper

For the salsa
1 red onion, finely diced
1 red pepper, cored, deseeded
   and finely diced
2 banana shallots, finely diced
75g salted anchovies,
   the best you can find,
   roughly chopped
Finely grated zest of 2 lemons
2 garlic cloves, grated
1 tablespoon finely
   chopped sage
1 teaspoon finely chopped
   rosemary leaves

Preheat the oven to 190°C/Gas Mark 5. Lay a wide strip of tin foil on a baking tray. Drizzle it with olive oil. Place the red peppers on top of the foil and season. Cover with a second strip of tin foil and then seal tightly around the edges to form a bag. Roast for 45 minutes, remove from the oven and let the peppers cool in the bag. The peppers will steam a little and create some condensation that is all flavour.

. . . . .

Warm a splash of olive oil in a large, heavy-bottomed saucepan over a medium heat. Add the onions and cook for about 15 minutes, until soft, stirring from time to time. Add the garlic and cook for 2–3 minutes, then add the chillies and stir. Throw in the sugar and saffron, then the pastis and vinegar, and cook on a medium heat until the liquid has evaporated and you have a pan full of lovely saffron-coloured onions.

. . . . .

Empty the bag of red peppers into the pan, along with all the steamed juices. Cover with the stock, bring to the boil, reduce the heat and simmer very gently for 25–30 minutes. Add the double cream, bring to the boil, then remove from the heat.

. . . . .

Cool slightly then whizz in a blender or food processor until smooth. Pass through a fine sieve into a container and season to taste with salt and cayenne pepper. At this stage, you can refrigerate the soup for up to a couple of days and heat it up when needed.

. . . . .

When you are ready to serve, mix together all of the ingredients for the salsa in a bowl. Taste and season. Bring the soup to the boil and ladle it into warmed serving bowls. Spoon some salsa into each bowl and trickle on some olive oil just before serving.

Photographs overleaf

Earthy, strong flavours dominate this soup. The longer you roast the garlic, the sweeter and deeper in flavour it becomes. The onions, garlic and lemon are all cooked together in a foil bag for several hours – stick it in the oven, forget about it and wait for the house to fill with amazing smells.

Garlic & brown bread soup

SERVES 4

Extra virgin olive oil,
  for cooking
3 whole garlic heads,
  halved horizontally
6 onions, quartered
  lengthways
2 lemons
1 bunch of thyme
1 litre chicken stock
200ml double cream
3–4 slices of good brown
  bread, roughly torn
100g butter
Handful of parsley,
  tough stems discarded,
  finely chopped
3 tablespoons small
  capers, drained
Salt and freshly ground
  black pepper

Preheat the oven to 150°C/Gas Mark 2.

.....

Lay a length of tin foil on a large baking tray. Drizzle generously with olive oil. Place the garlic on the foil with the onions. Add the whole lemons and the thyme. Season and drizzle over another generous amount of olive oil. Place a sheet of tin foil over the top and seal tightly all around the sides to form a bag. Bake for 3–4 hours, until everything is cooked and soft. Remove from the oven and leave to cool in the foil bag.

.....

Gently lift the lemons from the bag and set aside. Squeeze all the cloves of garlic from the heads into a large bowl. Add the onions and drain any liquid from the bag on top. Discard the thyme sprigs. Mash the onion and garlic together with a fork.

.....

In a large, heavy-bottomed saucepan, warm a couple of tablespoons of olive oil over a medium heat. Add the onion and garlic 'mash' and cook, stirring now and again, for 4–5 minutes. Add the chicken stock and bring to the boil. Pour in the double cream and then add the brown bread. Remove from the heat, stir, and let the bread sit and thicken the soup for 20–25 minutes.

.....

Bring back to the boil, remove from the heat, then whizz in a blender or food processor until smooth. Pass through a fine sieve into a clean pan and season.

.....

Cut the reserved lemons in half, cut off the ends, then scoop out the membrane and pips and discard them. Cut the peel and remaining flesh into 1cm chunks.

.....

Heat a large frying pan over a high heat and drizzle in a little olive oil. Throw in the chopped lemon and cook until it starts to tinge and take on some colour. Drain on kitchen paper and return the pan to the heat. Add the butter and cook until it starts to go brown. Just as it turns a rich, nutty brown, put the lemon pieces back into the pan. Add the parsley and capers, stir and season.

.....

Bring the soup back up to the boil and pour into warmed serving bowls. Garnish with the lemon butter and serve.

Photograph overleaf

The best way to describe this broth is rich, meaty and substantial. It takes a while to cook, but trust me, it's worth the wait and it'll keep for a few days sealed in the fridge after it's been cooked. I think butter beans are an under used pulse. They have loads of character and take on lush flavours from everything they're cooked with.

Butter bean & bacon broth

SERVES 4-6

300g dried butter beans
400g piece of whole,
  smoked streaky bacon
8 thyme sprigs
1 whole garlic head,
  halved horizontally
2 celery sticks, tough strings
  removed, trimmed
1 potato, peeled but left whole
1 Spanish onion, halved
4 cloves
2 lemons
50g caster sugar
Handful of curly-leaf parsley,
  leaves picked and chopped;
  the stalks tied together in a
  bundle with kitchen string
Salt and freshly ground
  black pepper

Put the butter beans in a large bowl, cover with cold water and leave overnight in the fridge.
. . . . .
The next day, drain the beans and place them in a large casserole or heavy-bottomed saucepan. Cover with fresh water, bring to the boil and immediately drain them again in a colander in the sink. Put the beans back into the pan and cover with about 15cm water.
. . . . .
Carefully remove the rind from the bacon – try to keep the rind in one piece. Place the thyme on the bacon rind and roll it up like a Swiss roll. Tie it up with kitchen string and stick it into the pot of beans. Pop the garlic halves into the pan with the whole piece of bacon, celery sticks and potato. Stud the onion halves with the cloves and put them into the pot too. Bring to the boil. Turn the heat down to a gentle simmer and cook, uncovered, for 2½ hours (keep an eye on it and top up with a little boiling water if it looks too thick), or until the beans are soft and the bacon is cooked.
. . . . .
With a potato peeler, pare the zest from the lemons in long strips, taking care not to remove any of the bitter white pith. Finely slice the zest into little strips. Juice the lemons and mix the juice with the sugar in a small saucepan. Warm, stirring, until the sugar has dissolved. Put the lemon strips in another small pan, cover with water and bring to the boil. When the zest is just soft, drain it in a sieve then place it in the juice syrup.
. . . . .

When the broth is cooked, remove the bacon rind, celery, onion, potato, whole bacon and garlic. Discard the rind, celery and onion, but keep the potato, whole bacon and garlic. Place the potato in a mixing bowl and squeeze the cloves of garlic from their skins into the bowl. Add a little of the cooking liquid and mash together with a fork or whisk until smooth.

·····

Bring the broth back to the boil and whisk in the potato mixture. This will thicken the soup. Turn off the heat. Place the bundle of parsley stalks in the soup and leave to infuse like a cup of tea for 5 minutes, then remove.

·····

Flake up the cooked bacon and add it to the soup with the chopped parsley. Drain the confit lemon strips and add them too. Season and serve in warmed bowls. This is so good!

A classic soup from our set lunch menu at the pub, this is a firm favourite with the chefs as it's easy to make but full of flavour. I like to use Crown Prince pumpkin for its flavour but any other British squash variety would work well.

Pumpkin soup with oyster mushrooms

SERVES 4

3 tablespoons vegetable oil
75g butter
1 onion, finely diced
15g dried mushrooms
½ Crown Prince pumpkin, peeled, deseeded and cut into 3cm chunks – you will need about 700g pumpkin flesh
800ml chicken stock
100ml double cream
3 tablespoons pumpkin seeds
200g oyster mushrooms, halved
150g blue cheese, such as Stilton or Roquefort
4 teaspoons pumpkin seed oil
Salt and freshly ground black pepper

In a large, heavy-bottomed saucepan, warm a little of the vegetable oil and melt 25g of the butter over a medium heat. Add the onion and a pinch of salt. Sweat gently until soft, stirring from time to time, for about 10–15 minutes, then add the dried mushrooms and cook for a further 5 minutes until the mushrooms have softened and released some flavour.
. . . . .
Add the chunks of pumpkin and pour in the chicken stock. Turn the heat up and bring to the boil. Reduce the heat and cook at a gentle simmer until the pumpkin is soft – about 30 minutes.
. . . . .
Pour in the double cream and bring to the boil. Remove the pan from the heat, cool slightly, then blend the soup in a blender or food processor until smooth – you may not need all of the cooking liquid so add it a bit at a time until you have the texture you like. Pass the soup through a fine sieve, season and keep warm.
. . . . .
Preheat the oven to 180°C/Gas Mark 4. Place the pumpkin seeds on a baking sheet and toast them for 5–8 minutes until a little tinged. Remove to a plate to cool.
. . . . .
Melt the remaining butter in a large, heavy-bottomed frying pan over a medium–high heat and fry the oyster mushrooms until cooked and just beginning to take on a little colour. When they're ready, transfer them to a plate.
. . . . .
Pour the hot soup into warmed serving bowls, crumble over the blue cheese and scatter over the mushrooms. Sprinkle with the toasted pumpkin seeds, drizzle on the pumpkin oil and serve.

Cauliflower cheese in soup form. This is rich and velvety, so the capers add a welcome bite of salt and acidity. The better the cheese you use, the better the soup will taste.

Cauliflower & Cheddar soup with capers

SERVES 4

50g butter
1 onion, diced
2 garlic cloves, grated
1 large or 2 small cauliflowers,
    broken into florets
About 1 litre chicken stock
200ml double cream
200g strong Cheddar cheese,
    the best you can find,
    finely grated
½ teaspoon paprika
Salt

For the capers
Vegetable oil, for deep-frying
4 tablespoons large capers,
    drained from the vinegar
    but vinegar reserved

In a large, heavy-bottomed saucepan, melt the butter over a medium heat. Add the onion, garlic and a pinch of salt and cook until soft – about 10–15 minutes.

.....

Reserve some of the smallest cauliflower florets for garnish, then add the rest to the onions. Cover with about 750ml chicken stock (reserve the rest), turn the heat up and bring to the boil. Reduce the heat and simmer for 5–10 minutes until the cauliflower is soft.

.....

Add the cream, cheese and paprika. Bring the soup back to the boil, then remove from the heat and whizz in a blender or food processor until smooth. Pass through a fine sieve and season. If the soup seems a bit thick, thin it slightly with the reserved chicken stock until you get the consistency you like.

.....

For the capers, heat the vegetable oil in a deep fat fryer to 180°C. Pat the capers dry on some kitchen paper. Fry them until they pop and are very crisp. Remove from the oil with a slotted spoon and drain on kitchen paper. Season with salt.

.....

Place the reserved cauliflower florets in the reserved caper jar vinegar and leave to sit for a minute or two. Drain.

.....

Heat the soup and pour into warmed serving bowls. Sprinkle the deep-fried capers and the fast-pickled florets over the top of each bowl – in rows if you want to be a bit fancy – and serve immediately.

This soup is so simple. It has just a few ingredients and is easy to make, but it has a real depth of flavour. And it's proper warming too. If soups could give you a hug...

Butternut squash & Parmesan soup

100g butter
1 onion, diced
2 garlic cloves, grated
1kg butternut squash, peeled,
    halved, deseeded and cut
    into 2cm dice – you will
    need about 500g of flesh
800ml chicken stock
175g Parmesan cheese, grated
2 tablespoons truffle oil
200g fresh cep mushrooms,
    sliced if large; smaller
    ones left whole
1 x 200g packet of vacuum-
    packed chestnuts
10 sage leaves, chopped
Salt and freshly ground
    black pepper

Melt 50g of the butter in a large, heavy-bottomed saucepan over a medium–low heat, add the diced onion and sweat gently for about 10–15 minutes until soft, stirring from time to time.
.....

Add the garlic and cook for a further 2–3 minutes, then stir in the squash. Cover with the chicken stock, bring the pan to the boil, then turn the heat down to a gentle simmer. Cook for about 30 minutes, until the squash is soft.
.....

Remove from the heat, stir in the Parmesan and truffle oil and season. Purée in a blender or food processor then pass through a fine sieve into a clean saucepan and keep warm. If you're not eating the soup immediately, you can keep it in the fridge, in a sealed container, for a couple of days.
.....

In a frying pan, melt the remaining butter over a medium–high heat and fry the ceps until they are caramelised and brown. Add the chestnuts and cook for a further 2–3 minutes, then stir in all but about 2 teaspoons of the sage, keeping the rest for garnish.
.....

Pour the soup into warmed serving bowls. Spoon a bit of the cep and chestnut mixture over the top of each then sprinkle with the reserved sage. Serve immediately.

fish mains

I've got to be honest, I'm not one of life's natural fishermen. I grew up in Gloucestershire then worked in London – about as far from a boat as you can get! But whenever people ask me, 'If you weren't a chef, what would you be?' I always think I'd be a fisherman.

For a start, all the fishermen I've ever met are great blokes, the kind of people I really enjoy spending time with. And I love the idea of fishing: working really hard, the camaraderie of being away on the boat and bringing back a catch. There's a pride in that. I do think that when people complain about how much fish costs, they should reflect a moment on where it comes from and how fishermen risk their lives to get it to their table.

As a chef, I love the seasonality of fish and the quality of the cold-water fish from around the British Isles is amazing; it has great texture and flavour. If you can, find a good local fishmonger with a high turnover and buy the freshest fish. Alternatively, these days it's possible to buy excellent, sustainably sourced fish and seafood directly from the coast by mail order too.

Whether it's a dish as simple as Red mullet on baked Provençal vegetables or something a little more complex like Sea bass with black grape sauce, what I'm trying to do with the recipes here is to bring out the natural taste and texture of the fish. It's a question of lifting and enhancing it. Everyone knows pairing lemon with seafood is a classic, but why? The lemon is adding an acidity that will make the other flavours sparkle. I look for other ways to do the same in all my dishes, by finding the ingredient that punches up the flavour – it can be vinegar, verjus, capers, lime, or even a nice, crisp apple.

What I'm saying is that I'm giving you the security blanket of some of my favourite recipes here, but I hope you'll experiment, hone your skills, and find your own favourite combinations.

This is my take on that 1970s pub classic, smartened up a bit with the lovely, meaty monkfish and a proper lemony mayonnaise. It's worth tracking down the semolina and tapioca flours as they make a super-crunchy coating. You'll probably want to try it on all kinds of other fish or even vegetables, such as broccoli or courgette flowers. Scampi makes a nice, casual lunch or you can serve it as a starter or a canapé that's guaranteed to please a crowd.

Monkfish scampi

SERVES 4

Groundnut, vegetable or
   other flavourless oil,
   for deep-frying
200g semolina flour, plus
   a little more for dusting
100g tapioca flour
½ teaspoon bicarbonate
   of soda
Cayenne pepper, to taste
330ml sparkling water
500g monkfish, cut into
   3–5cm cubes
Salt
Finely grated zest of
   1 large lemon, to garnish

For the lemon mayo
3 egg yolks
1 tablespoon white
   wine vinegar
1 tablespoon Dijon mustard
Juice of 1 large lemon
500ml vegetable oil
Freshly ground white pepper

First make the lemon mayonnaise. Whizz the egg yolks, vinegar, mustard and lemon juice in a food processor. With the motor still running, slowly pour in the oil through the feed tube, processing until the mayonnaise is emulsified and thickened. If it's too thick, thin it slightly with some warm water. Season with salt and white pepper and refrigerate until needed.

.....

When you're ready to eat, slowly heat the oil in a deep fat fryer until it reaches 180°C.

.....

While the oil is warming up, quickly whisk together the batter. Put the flours and bicarbonate of soda into a bowl. Season with salt and cayenne pepper. Pour in the sparkling water and whisk to form a loose batter.

.....

Dust the pieces of monkfish in some semolina flour and then dip them in the batter. Fry for 3–4 minutes or until the batter is crisp and golden. Don't crowd the fryer. You may need to do this in batches – make sure you let the oil come back up to temperature between batches. Use a slotted spoon to remove the monkfish from the oil. Drain on kitchen paper and season with salt and cayenne pepper, to taste.

.....

Serve with the lemon mayonnaise, garnished with lemon zest.

This is a great alternative to the beef pasty. The smoking and curing process gives smoked haddock a meatier texture than most fish so it can withstand a longer cooking time. It also works with swede and black pepper – key pasty ingredients.

Smoked haddock pasties

SERVES 4

250g swede (about
½ swede), peeled
200g waxy new potatoes,
peeled (or scrubbed Jersey
Royals would be perfect)
1 onion, diced
4 tablespoons chopped
flat-leaf parsley
1 tablespoon cracked black
pepper (more if you really
like pepper)
500g smoked haddock, skin
and pin bones removed,
cut into 1cm dice
4 knobs of butter
1 egg, plus 1 egg yolk,
lightly beaten, to glaze
Flaky sea salt, to finish
Brown sauce, to serve
(optional)
Salt

For the pastry
750g strong bread flour,
plus a little more
for dusting
1½ teaspoons salt
100g chilled lard, diced
75g chilled butter, diced
220–260ml water, chilled

Start with the pastry. Put the flour and salt into the bowl of a stand mixer with the lard and butter. Using the beater attachment, mix together on a medium speed. When it starts to look like breadcrumbs, change the attachment to a dough hook and add 3–4 tablespoons of the cold water. Mix, slowly adding more water to form a dough – you will need to gradually add about another 160–200ml water, just until you get the consistency of a firm bread dough. Once it's come together, continue to knead with the dough hook for 4–5 minutes until it's smooth and quite elastic. Remove from the bowl and wrap in cling film. Rest in the fridge for at least 1 hour, or up to a day.
.....

While the dough is resting, slice the swede and potatoes into 3–5mm slices. I've always been told that the potato and swede must be sliced not diced in a pasty so I'm not going to change now! Place the sliced vegetables in a bowl with the onion, parsley, black pepper and a pinch of salt. Stir in the smoked haddock.
.....

Preheat the oven to 180°C/Gas Mark 4. Line a baking tray with baking parchment. Divide the rested dough into four equal pieces. Shape each piece into a ball. Lightly dust a surface with a little flour and roll out each ball into a rough circle, about 25cm in diameter. Spoon a quarter of the filling on to a disc of pastry. Spread the filling on to one half of the disc, leaving the other half clear. Stick a knob of butter on top of the filling. Brush the edges lightly with water then carefully fold the pastry over and join the edges. Push together with your fingers to seal. Crimp the edges to make sure the filling is held securely inside. You can seal it with a fork or make small twists along the edges and then fold the end corners underneath. Repeat with the rest of the pastry and filling.
.....

Put the pasties on the lined baking tray. Brush the top of each one with the beaten egg and sprinkle with a little flaky sea salt. Bake for 40 minutes, until golden brown. Cool on the tray for 10 minutes before serving, with brown sauce if you like.

Sea bream, sometimes called gilthead bream, is usually farmed, which makes it a good, sustainable choice. I love sea bream. Baking it whole like this helps to keep it tasty and moist, and it's also so easy to do.

Roast sea bream with white beans & bacon

SERVES 2

2 x 450–500g sea bream, scaled, gutted and gills removed (you can ask your fishmonger to do this)
Salt and freshly ground white pepper

For the fish rub
4 tablespoons olive oil
1 tablespoon flaky sea salt
2 teaspoons smoked paprika
2 teaspoons fennel seeds
1 teaspoon garlic powder
1 teaspoon dried sage
1 teaspoon dried rosemary

For the white beans and bacon
100g dried white beans, such as cannellini beans
250g whole piece of Alsace bacon, or other strongly smoked, streaky bacon, skin removed but reserved
150ml extra virgin olive oil, plus a little more for frying
1 onion, finely diced
2 garlic cloves, grated
½ teaspoon cayenne pepper
½ teaspoon smoked paprika
6 rosemary sprigs, tied together with kitchen string
1 lemon, rind thinly pared in strips, any white pith removed
200ml chicken stock

To make the white bean and bacon sauce, first soak the dried white beans overnight in cold water.

.....

The next day, drain the beans, put them into a large saucepan and cover with fresh water. Bring the liquid to the boil then turn it down to a simmer. Add the Alsace bacon skin and gently cook the beans until they are soft and tender. This should take about 1½ hours – keep an eye on them and add a little boiling water from the kettle if the level gets a bit low. Drain the beans and discard the bacon skin.

.....

Dice the Alsace bacon into lardons. Warm a little of the olive oil in a heavy-bottomed saucepan over a medium–high heat and fry the lardons until they're brown and crisp. Remove the bacon from the pan with a slotted spoon and drain on some kitchen paper. Reduce the heat under the pan to medium–low, add the onion and garlic and sweat for about 10–15 minutes, until soft, stirring from time to time.

.....

Add the cayenne pepper, smoked paprika, rosemary and lemon rind. Keep a quarter of the drained white beans back to add later, then tip the rest into the pan. Pour in the chicken stock and 150ml olive oil and bring to the boil. Reduce the heat to low and gently simmer for 30–40 minutes.

.....

Remove the rosemary and lemon rind and then purée the sauce in a blender or food processor until smooth. Season and pass through a fine sieve. Add the lardons and the reserved, whole white beans. Keep to one side.

.....

Continues overleaf

Roast sea bream with white beans & bacon
Continued

For the shallot reduction
10 banana shallots,
    finely sliced
300ml white wine
300ml white wine vinegar
2 tablespoons caster sugar
3 tablespoons finely
    chopped tarragon
2 teaspoons cracked
    black pepper

To make the shallot reduction, put the shallots in a large saucepan with the wine, vinegar and sugar. Bring to the boil and then turn the heat down to a gentle simmer and cook until the shallots are translucent and the liquid has evaporated – keep an eye on it and remove from the heat as soon as the liquid has gone so that the shallots don't catch on the bottom. Leave to cool and then stir in the tarragon and black pepper.

.....

Preheat the oven to 220°C/Gas Mark 7. Line a roasting tin with baking parchment.

.....

Mix together all of the fish rub ingredients to make a rough paste. Make 3–4 incisions into each side of the sea bream, being careful not to cut too deeply into the flesh. Rub the mix into the fish, making sure you cover all the skin.

.....

Put the fish into the lined tin and place in the oven for 7–8 minutes. Turn the fish over and return the tin to the oven to cook for a further 7–8 minutes. The flesh should flake away from the bone easily.

.....

While the fish is cooking, warm the white beans and bacon and pour it into a large serving bowl. Heat up some shallot reduction and spoon it into the middle of two serving plates and then put a whole fish on top. Spoon over a little of the white beans and bacon and serve the fish, with the bowl of remaining beans in the middle of the table.

The rich, woodland flavour of dried mushrooms works beautifully with the meaty texture of brill. The purée is so simple and fresh, you don't even have to cook it and it's very versatile – give it a go with poultry and pork too. It will keep in the fridge for three to four days. This recipe is quite straightforward, but it's a good idea to read it through before you get cracking as towards the end you need to do a few things at once.

Brill with mushroom purée

SERVES 4

30g dried trompette
    mushrooms or other
    richly flavoured
    dried mushrooms
300g button
    mushrooms, sliced
½ teaspoon flaky sea salt
Juice of 1 lemon
250ml double cream
12 asparagus spears
100ml water
80g butter
4 x 150g fillet portions
    of brill, skinned
Cayenne pepper, to taste
Vegetable oil, for frying
2 tablespoons cider vinegar
6 tablespoons rapeseed oil
1 Granny Smith apple,
    unpeeled, cored and
    finely diced
2 tablespoons finely
    chopped chives
2 tablespoons finely
    diced cornichons
Salt

First, soak half the dried mushrooms in just enough boiling water to cover them. Leave them to cool in the water while you continue preparing the dish. In a spice grinder or using a pestle and mortar, grind the remaining mushrooms to a fine powder.
.....
To make the mushroom purée, place the sliced button mushrooms in a bowl and sprinkle on the flaky sea salt and half the lemon juice. Mix together and leave to cure for 20 minutes, then put them in a clean tea towel and squeeze out the excess moisture.
.....
Pour the double cream into a saucepan and bring to the boil over a medium heat. Stir in the button mushrooms and remove from the heat. Leave to cook in the residual heat for 5 minutes, then purée in a blender or food processor until smooth. Season with salt and pass through a fine sieve. Keep warm, or alternatively if you are making this ahead, keep covered in the fridge until needed – it will keep for 3–4 days.
.....
To prepare the asparagus, cut the ends off the woody stalks and peel the lower parts of the stems. Place the water and 60g of the butter in a shallow frying pan and bring to the boil. Add a pinch of salt, then the asparagus, and cook for 3–4 minutes until just tender when pierced with a small, sharp knife.
.....
At the same time, prepare the brill by pushing one side of each fillet into the blitzed mushroom powder and then shaking off any excess. Season with salt and cayenne pepper, to taste.
.....
Continues overleaf

Brill with mushroom purée

Continued

Heat a little vegetable oil in a large, non-stick frying pan over a medium heat. Place the brill fillets in the pan, black-side down, and gently fry for 3–4 minutes until almost cooked all of the way through. Add the rest of the butter and the remaining lemon juice to the pan, turn the fish over, baste in the lemon juice and butter and cook for a further minute.

.....

To make the mushroom dressing, drain the soaked mushrooms and chop them finely with a sharp knife. Put them in a small saucepan with the cider vinegar. Quickly bring to the boil and then remove from the heat. Add the rapeseed oil, apple and chives.

.....

To serve, spread a big spoonful of the warm mushroom purée on to a warmed serving plate with the back of a spoon. Sprinkle over some cornichons and place the asparagus on top. Put a piece of fish on top of the asparagus and then dress with the mushroom dressing. Repeat with the rest of the brill fillets and serve immediately.

This is a fantastic dish that makes you think of sunshine even when it's cold and grey outside. A true taste of Provence, it's full of classic Mediterranean flavours that have such warmth and are a big hit with pretty much everyone. The vegetable base can be made up a day in advance and then finished in the oven with the fish on top the next day.

Red mullet on baked Provençal vegetables

SERVES 4

2 large aubergines
8 ripe tomatoes
3 large courgettes,
    cut into 5mm slices
Olive oil, for drizzling
4 x 170g red mullet fillets,
    pin-boned and scaled
1 teaspoon lemon thyme
    leaves (ordinary thyme
    if lemon isn't available)
1 teaspoon oregano leaves
Flaky sea salt, to finish
Salt and freshly ground
    black pepper

For the onion jam
3½ tablespoons olive oil
3½ tablespoons red
    wine vinegar
500g red onions,
    halved and sliced
1 tablespoon thyme leaves
1 tablespoon light
    muscovado sugar
3 garlic cloves, grated
Finely grated zest of
    1 lemon

Pierce the aubergines all over with a sharp knife, put them on to a plate and cover with cling film. Microwave them on full power for 8–10 minutes until they are very soft in the middle. If you don't have a microwave, place the pierced aubergines on a baking tray and bake at 200°C/Gas Mark 6 for 45 minutes–1 hour, depending on their size. Keep an eye on them, as you want them to be just fluffy in the middle and for the flesh to be as pale as possible. Cool then cut them in half lengthways, scoop out the flesh, mash with a fork and season.
.....

Make the onion jam. Pour the olive oil and vinegar into a large saucepan with the onions, thyme and sugar and cook over a medium heat for 40–50 minutes, until the onions are soft and have an almost jammy consistency. Stir from time to time and make sure the mixture doesn't catch on the bottom. Remove from the heat and add the garlic and lemon zest. Mix the onion jam into the mashed-up aubergine and spoon this into the bottom of an ovenproof serving dish.
.....

Preheat the oven to 180°C/Gas Mark 4. Prepare a bowl of iced water and place it by the hob. Bring a large saucepan of water to the boil and drop in the tomatoes – count to ten then remove and plunge them into the iced water. Peel the skins from the tomatoes and slice them into 5mm slices. Layer the tomatoes and courgettes on top of the aubergine and onion mixture in lines, or one by one, or just randomly. Drizzle on some olive oil and season. Bake for 10–12 minutes.
.....

Remove from the oven and put the fillets of red mullet on top, skin-side up. Return to the oven and bake for 8–10 minutes until the fish is cooked. Sprinkle on the lemon thyme and oregano and season with flaky sea salt. Serve immediately.

This is a fantastically simple dish, but don't be deceived – it has a very complex flavour. Verjus is a ripe grape juice that has a lovely gentle, sweet-tart acidity to it that cuts through the richness of the butter in this sauce. You can also use it in salad dressings and marinades. The hake needs nothing more than some simply steamed new potatoes as an accompaniment.

Hake with verjus butter

SERVES 4

Flaky sea salt, for sprinkling
1 side of hake, about
   400–500g, skinned
   and pin-boned (you can
   ask your fishmonger
   to do this for you)
1 jar or vac-pack of vine
   leaves in brine
Olive oil, for cooking the fish
2 banana shallots,
   finely diced
100ml white wine
75ml white wine vinegar
2 tablespoons double cream
100g chilled butter,
   cut into cubes
20ml verjus
Cayenne pepper, to taste
200g green seedless
   grapes, halved
Salt
Steamed new potatoes,
   to serve

Roll out a large sheet of cling film and sprinkle a small layer of flaky sea salt on top. Place the hake on top and then sprinkle over a little more salt. Wrap the fish tightly in cling film, put on a tray and refrigerate for 1½ hours. This process draws moisture from the fish, firms up the flesh and seasons it.

.....

Next, wash off the salt and pat the fish dry with kitchen paper. Divide the fish into four equal portions. Remove the vine leaves from the packet or jar and cut out any thick pieces of stalk. Wrap each piece of fish in the vine leaves, making sure that there are no gaps, then wrap each one tightly in cling film to help set the leaves in place. Put the fish into the fridge to firm up for at least 2 hours, or overnight.

.....

Preheat the oven to 170°C/Gas Mark 3. When you're ready to cook the fish, gently remove the portions from the cling film, put them on a baking tray and trickle on some olive oil. Bake for 12–15 minutes until the fish is cooked – it should feel firm but still have some give in it when pressed with your thumb.

.....

While the fish is cooking, make the sauce. Put the shallots in a small saucepan with the wine and vinegar and simmer on a medium–high heat until reduced to a glaze. When most of the liquid has evaporated, pour in the cream and bring to the boil. Reduce the heat and slowly whisk in the diced butter, one piece at a time, allowing each cube of butter to be amalgamated before adding another. Be careful not to let the sauce boil or it will split.

.....

When all of the butter has been added, add the verjus and season with salt and cayenne pepper. Remove from the heat, place the grapes in the sauce and leave them to warm through gently for 1–2 minutes. Place the hake on warmed plates and spoon over the sauce. Serve immediately, with some steamed new potatoes.

Mackerel is full of flavour, with a taste of the sea – it's also one of the best British fish around and is in good supply. The sea herbs I use here are a tasty addition but if you can't find them, simply use the same quantity of spinach, sorrel, rehydrated dried seaweeds or leafy garden herbs instead. Serve the fish with a potato salad or some plain rice with a few more sea herbs stirred through it.

Seaside stuffed mackerel

100g samphire, picked over
75g sea purslane, picked over
65g fresh breadcrumbs
40g sea aster, chopped
4 salted anchovies, chopped
3 tablespoons creamed horseradish
2 tablespoons Dijon mustard
Juice and zest of 1 lemon
8 medium mackerel, filleted and v-boned to remove all the pin bones (you could ask your fishmonger to do this for you)
Vegetable or olive oil, for cooking
Salt and freshly ground black pepper

For the sauce
100g butter
Juice and zest of 1 lemon
1 garlic clove, grated
2 tablespoons chopped parsley (flat-leaf or curly-leaf, according to preference)

In a mixing bowl, stir together the samphire, purslane, breadcrumbs, sea aster, anchovies, horseradish, mustard and the lemon juice and zest to form a loose paste – you may need to add a splash or two of water. Season to taste.
.....
Place the mackerel fillets skin-side down on a chopping board and divide the stuffing mixture between half the fillets, spooning it over the flesh and spreading it evenly. Then put the other half of the mackerel fillets on top. Tie them together with kitchen string to re-form them to look roughly like fish. Place them on a plate, cover with cling film and refrigerate for about 1 hour to firm up.
.....
When you're ready to cook the mackerel, brush the fish with a little oil and cook under a hot grill or on a hot barbecue for 3–4 minutes per side until the skin is crisp and the flesh is cooked through. Alternatively, place a large, heavy frying pan over a medium heat and cook for 5 minutes per side. You may need to cook them in batches.
.....
While the fish is cooking, make the sauce. Heat the butter in a small saucepan until it foams and turns a rich, golden brown. Add the lemon juice and zest, the garlic and then the parsley. Season and spoon on top of the fish.

The proper name for this kind of dish is 'grenobloise', meaning it comes from the town of Grenoble in southern France. It's usually garnished with lemon, parsley, capers and breadcrumbs or croutons and it's a combination that's perfectly suited to fish. Here I've used lemon sole, but the dish is just as good with cod, John Dory or any other robust, white fish. This is very simple, clean cooking that's all about last-minute assembly – classic and delicious.

Lemon sole with parsley sauce

SERVES 2

3 slices of brown bread, crusts removed, cut into 5mm cubes
Olive oil, for drizzling and frying
2 tablespoons small capers in brine, drained and patted dry
1 lemon
2 lemon sole, skinned both sides and trimmed (ask your fishmonger to do this for you)
Plain flour, for dusting
50g butter
4 tablespoons finely chopped curly-leaf parsley
Salt and freshly ground white pepper

For the parsley sauce
1 bunch of curly-leaf parsley, leaves picked from the stems and stems discarded
25g butter, plus a little more for smoothing out the sauce
2 banana shallots, finely diced
100ml white wine
100ml double cream

For the chard
2 large Swiss chard stalks
75ml water
25g butter

Preheat the oven to 180°C/Gas Mark 4.
.....
Place the cubes of bread on a baking tray. Drizzle with a little olive oil and bake until they are toasted and crisp, about 8–10 minutes. Remove from the oven and season.
.....
Warm 1–2cm of olive oil in the bottom of a deep, medium-sized saucepan until hot. Carefully lower in the capers on a slotted spoon and cook for a few minutes until they are crisp and start to pop. Remove them with the slotted spoon and drain on kitchen paper.
.....
Trim the ends from the lemon and stand upright on a chopping board. With a small, sharp knife work your way around the fruit, cutting away the peel and outer membrane. Cut the fleshy segments out of the inner membrane. Squeeze the inner membrane's juice into a glass and reserve it for cooking the fish. Lay the lemon segments on a roasting tray and blowtorch them until they are charred and blackened – this will give them a lovely, toasted taste.
.....
Next, make the parsley sauce. Prepare a bowl of iced water and put it by the hob. Bring a saucepan of salted water to the boil and blanch the parsley leaves until they're just wilted, about 5 seconds. Drain and immediately plunge into the iced water to refresh, then drain and squeeze out the excess water with some kitchen paper. Put on to a chopping board and chop roughly.
.....
Warm the butter in a small, heavy-bottomed saucepan, add the shallots and sweat over a medium–low heat until soft, stirring from time to time. Pour on the wine and bring to the boil. Boil until reduced to a glaze then pour in the double cream.
.....

Bring to the boil, add the blanched parsley, stir and season. Remove from the heat and immediately whizz in a blender or food processor until smooth – you may need to add an extra knob of butter to help smooth out the sauce. Pass through a fine sieve, cover and keep warm, or store in the fridge until needed if you are making the sauce a few hours ahead.

.....

To prepare the chard, tear the green leafy part from the top of the stalks and finely slice them into strips. Portion up the stalks into pieces about 4cm long and trim any brown bits from them. Put the water and butter together in a small saucepan and bring to the boil. Add a pinch of salt and the chard stalks. Turn the heat down and gently cook them until they just start to go soft, about 4–5 minutes. Stir in the thinly sliced leaves and cook until just wilted; this should take no more than a minute. Drain, transfer to a serving dish and keep warm.

.....

Heat a little olive oil in a large frying pan over a medium heat. Dust the fish on both sides with flour and shake off any excess. Place the fish in the pan and cook for 2–3 minutes, until they get a crisp, golden brown crust. Flip the fish over and cook for a further 2–3 minutes. Drop in the butter and when it has melted, baste the fish with it. Add the reserved lemon juice to the pan and baste the fish a little more. Remove the fish from the pan and throw in the chopped parsley, croutons, capers and lemon segments. Season.

.....

Heat up the parsley sauce and drizzle it on to two warmed plates. Place the lemon sole on top, then pour on the garnishes from the fish pan. Serve immediately with the chard alongside.

Photograph overleaf

Sea bass is a fantastic round fish with a firm but flaky flesh which makes a great contrast to its crisp, cooked skin. Poaching the celery heart is a super way to use the end of a head of celery and it pairs well with the rich and slightly sweet grape sauce, tasty fish and toasted hazelnuts.

Sea bass with black grape sauce & celery

SERVES 2

2 x 200g wild, line-caught
  sea bass fillets, skin on,
  pin bones removed
Plain flour, for dusting
Vegetable oil, for frying
  the fish
Knob of butter
Squeeze of lemon juice
25g toasted hazelnuts,
  roughly chopped or crushed
2 tablespoons hazelnut oil
Salt and freshly ground
  white pepper

For the black grape sauce
60g butter, plus a knob
  more for finishing
1 red onion, halved
  and finely sliced
175ml ruby port
75ml red wine
300g black seedless
  grapes, halved
30g blackberries
  (frozen is fine)
1 tablespoon redcurrant jelly

For the celery
1 small root end
  of a celery head
200ml water
2 tablespoons dessert wine
75g butter
1 teaspoon thyme leaves

To make the black grape sauce, put the butter into a saucepan and melt it over a medium heat. Add the red onion and sweat gently for approximately 10–15 minutes until soft, stirring from time to time. Pour in the port and red wine, then add the grapes, blackberries and redcurrant jelly. Bring to the boil, turn the heat down and simmer for 25–30 minutes, until the sauce has reduced by half. Remove from the heat.

·····

Blitz in a blender or food processor until smooth, pass through a fine sieve, season, and keep in the fridge until needed if not using immediately.

·····

To cook the celery, cut the root in half lengthways and trim any brown or dirty bits from it. Pick any leaves from the celery and reserve. Peel any tough strings from the celery heart halves with a vegetable peeler then place the heart in a high-sided frying pan. Pour in the water and dessert wine and add the butter. Season with a generous pinch of salt, place the pan on a medium–high heat and bring to the boil.

·····

Turn the heat down to a simmer and cook until the celery heart is soft, the cooking liquid has reduced and the butter and water have emulsified – this should take about 25 minutes. Baste the celery with the cooking liquid, stir in the thyme leaves and keep warm.

·····

With a sharp knife, cut a few incisions in the sea bass skin to prevent it from curling up during cooking. Don't cut too deeply into the flesh. Dust the sea bass flesh with flour and shake off any excess. Season with salt.

·····

Heat a large, non-stick frying pan over a medium heat and pour in a little vegetable oil. When hot, place the sea bass fillets in the pan, skin-side down, and hold them in place with your hand until you feel that they've relaxed and the skin no longer wants to curl up. Cook until the skin is crisp and the fish is cooked 90 per cent of the way through – this should take about 3–4 minutes. If you cook it over a medium heat, you will get a much better result and a crispy skin. If you cook it too high and fast, the skin will burn and cook unevenly.

·····

Flip the sea bass over, add the knob of butter to the pan and squeeze in the lemon juice. Baste the fish so it is ready to serve.

·····

Warm the grape sauce – you may want to stir in a knob of butter to enrich it. Pour a spoonful of the sauce (you won't need all of the sauce, but it freezes well so you can save any extra for another time) on to a warmed serving plate and place a sea bass fillet and a piece of celery heart on top. Sprinkle over half the toasted hazelnuts and drizzle on half the hazelnut oil. If you have any leaves left from the celery, garnish the top with them. Repeat with the other fillet then serve immediately.

Plaice is so versatile – it's fantastic deep-fried in batter, pan-fried, poached or roasted whole on the bone. If you get it in peak season, a jumbo plaice is a great and cost-effective substitute for brill or turbot. I use curly-leaf parsley here and in most of my fish recipes because it has a milder taste than flat-leaf parsley, which makes it a better match for the more delicate flavour of fish.

Plaice with caper sauce & roast fennel

SERVES 4

1 large plaice, about 800–900g
  (see right for preparation)
2–3 tablespoons vegetable,
  groundnut or other
  flavourless oil
3–4 fennel bulbs, tough
  outer leaves removed,
  quartered lengthways
1 onion, finely diced
2 garlic cloves, grated
330ml white wine
50ml pastis (anise-
  flavoured liqueur)
Splash of double cream
150g butter, cut into
  small cubes
Juice of 1 lemon
2 tablespoons finely chopped
  curly-leaf parsley
2 tablespoons finely chopped
  chervil
2 tablespoons capers
  in brine, drained
Salt and freshly ground
  black pepper

You'll need an ovenproof dish or roasting tin large enough to hold the whole fish. Trim the plaice with scissors, cutting off the fins and removing the gills and intestines. Scale the fish on both sides, then wash and pat it dry, or ask your fishmonger to prepare it for you.
.....
Preheat the oven to 180°C/Gas Mark 4. Warm a little of the oil in the dish or tin over a medium heat on the hob. Place the fennel in the dish – try not to move it about too much or it will stew rather than take on a lovely colour. When the fennel has a nice tinge all over – after about 5 minutes – lift it out of the dish and put aside. Pour a little more oil into the dish, reduce the heat a bit, add the onion and garlic and sweat gently for about 15 minutes, until soft, stirring from time to time. Return the fennel to the dish. Pour in the white wine and then put the plaice on top with its dark skin facing upwards.
.....
Put a lid on the dish or cover it tightly with foil. Place in the oven and bake for 15 minutes. Check it's cooked through by prodding the fish with a fork; the flesh should flake easily. Remove from the oven and carefully transfer the fennel and fish to a large, warm serving plate; cover with foil.
.....
Pass the liquid from the dish through a sieve into a saucepan. Place on the hob over a high heat, pour in the pastis and bring to the boil. Simmer the liquid down to a glaze and pour in the double cream. Reduce to a low heat and slowly whisk in the butter, allowing each cube to become incorporated before adding more, until you have a smooth sauce. Do not let it boil or it will split. When you have a lovely, velvety butter sauce, remove the pan from the heat, add the lemon juice, herbs and capers, and season.
.....
Remove the foil from the fish. Gently peel back the dark skin on the plaice and discard it. Spoon over the butter sauce and serve.

I love skate wings but they have a very short shelf life, which is why you don't often find them in supermarkets. Buy them as fresh as you can get them, from a fishmonger you trust. Roasting the chickpeas gives the dish a great crunchy texture. They also work well as a spicy, tasty snack served with a couple of cold beers.

Skate with crunchy chickpeas

SERVES 2

2 x 225g skate wings, skinned and trimmed (you can ask your fishmonger to do this for you)
Well-seasoned plain flour, for dusting
Vegetable oil, for frying
25g butter
Juice of ½ lemon

For the crunchy chickpeas
1 x 400g tin chickpeas, drained and rinsed
2 tablespoons olive oil
1 teaspoon ground cumin
1 teaspoon chilli powder
½ teaspoon cayenne pepper
½ teaspoon salt

For the chilli tomato sauce
6 ripe plum tomatoes
50ml red wine vinegar
1 teaspoon caster sugar
½ teaspoon chilli powder
2 red chillies, finely diced – seeds and all
2 tablespoons finely chopped marinated anchovies
Finely grated zest of 1 lemon
100ml olive oil
2 tablespoons finely chopped mint leaves

Preheat the oven to 180°C/Gas Mark 4.

. . . . .

Start with the chickpeas. In a large bowl, mix together the chickpeas, olive oil, cumin, chilli powder, cayenne pepper and salt. Make sure the chickpeas are well coated and spread them out evenly on a baking tray. Bake for 35–45 minutes until they are crunchy. Remove from the oven and cool.

. . . . .

Next make the chilli tomato sauce. Place a bowl of iced water next to the hob and bring a saucepan of water to the boil. Blanch 4 of the tomatoes in boiling water for 10 seconds and then immediately plunge them into the iced water to stop them cooking. Peel them and then cut them into quarters and remove the seeds. Pat the pieces of tomato dry on kitchen paper then chop them into small dice and reserve.

. . . . .

Whizz the remaining 2 tomatoes to a pulp in a blender or food processor. Pass through a fine sieve into a saucepan. Add the vinegar, sugar and chilli powder and boil over a high heat until reduced to a glaze. Remove the pan from the heat and stir in the fresh chillies, anchovies and lemon zest. Whisk in the olive oil and keep warm.

. . . . .

Dust both sides of the skate in the seasoned flour and shake off any excess. Warm a large, non-stick frying pan over a medium–high heat and pour in a little vegetable oil. Place the skate wings in the pan, thick-side down, and cook until browned and crisp – this will take about 4–5 minutes. Flip the fish over and cook for 2–3 minutes on the other side.

. . . . .

Continues overleaf

Skate with crunchy chickpeas

Continued

When cooked, remove from the pan. Add the butter and lemon juice to the pan and cook until the butter is foaming. Pour the foaming butter over the skate wings and leave to rest for 1–2 minutes.
.....

While the fish is resting, put the pan back on the heat and warm the chickpeas. Stir in the diced tomatoes and chilli tomato sauce then stir in the mint. Season with salt.
.....

Put the skate wings on to two warmed plates, then spoon over a generous amount of the chickpeas and chilli tomato sauce. Serve straight away.

Halibut is a hefty, thick fish which can take big flavours – I think of it as a fish for meat lovers. This is a big old lump of fish that I roast with garlic and thyme as if it's a rib of beef. The ragu is rich and luscious, perfect for a cold night in.

Halibut with chicken liver & mushroom ragu

SERVES 2

Vegetable oil, for cooking
1 x 500g tranche of halibut, skin on but scaled (you can ask your fishmonger to do this for you)
Large knob of butter
2 garlic cloves, skin on but crushed slightly
5 thyme sprigs
Salt and freshly ground white pepper

For the ragu
Vegetable oil, for cooking
100g lardons
200g chicken livers, trimmed and cleaned
200g cep mushrooms
1 carrot, finely diced
1 onion, finely diced
2 garlic cloves, grated
200ml Red wine sauce (see p. 290)
100ml ruby port
100g girolle mushrooms
1 tablespoon thyme leaves
100g chanterelle mushrooms
2 tablespoons finely chopped curly-leaf parsley
Splash of sherry vinegar
2–3 slices of brioche (it can be a day old)

First make the ragu. Warm a large, high-sided sauté pan or frying pan over a medium heat, pour in a little vegetable oil and fry the lardons until they're brown and their fat has rendered (run out into the pan). Remove from the pan with a slotted spoon and drain on a piece of kitchen paper.
.....
Using the same pan, with the pork fat still in it, raise the heat slightly and fry the chicken livers until they're browned and crisp. Don't move them around too much or they will stew rather than colour. When they're nice and brown, lift them from the pan with a slotted spoon on to the kitchen paper.
.....
Add a little more oil to the pan and fry the ceps until they take on some lovely colour all over, then remove them from the pan too. Drain on more kitchen paper.
.....
Next put the carrot, onion and garlic into the pan. Lower the heat slightly and sweat gently until soft – this will take about 5–6 minutes. Tip the lardons and ceps back into the pan and pour on the red wine sauce and port and bring to the boil. Reduce the heat and simmer gently for 4–5 minutes. Add the girolles and thyme leaves and cook for a further 5–6 minutes, until the ragu has reduced and is thick and rich. Stir in the chanterelles, the fried chicken livers and the parsley. Taste and season with salt, pepper and the sherry vinegar. Pour the ragu into a small, ovenproof dish.
.....
Continues overleaf

Halibut with chicken liver & mushroom ragu
Continued

For the spinach
20g butter
2 tablespoons olive oil
150g fresh, broad-leaf
spinach, tough stalks
removed, rinsed with
the water still clinging
to the leaves

Preheat the oven to 200°C/Gas Mark 6. Whizz the brioche slices in a food processor or blender until you have fine crumbs. Measure out 50g and sprinkle over the top of the ragu.
.....

Heat an ovenproof non-stick frying pan over a medium heat and pour in a little vegetable oil. Place the halibut in the pan, dark-skin down, and cook until it turns crisp – about 3 minutes. Flip it over and then add the knob of butter, garlic and thyme sprigs to the pan. Place the fish pan and ragu in the oven for 6–8 minutes until cooked and warmed through.
.....

While the fish is cooking, prepare the spinach. Heat a large saucepan over a medium heat. Add the butter and olive oil then stir in the spinach until wilted. Season and spread on a warmed serving dish.
.....

Remove the fish from the oven, baste it with its buttery cooking juices and season. Place the halibut on top of the spinach, spoon the mushroom ragu on to the dish and serve immediately.

meat mains

I'm very much at home with meat! There's no greater challenge and no bigger opportunity. The challenge is to get as much out of each cut as possible and the opportunity is to add great big whacks of flavour in the form of spice rubs, marinades, brines, loads of herbs and spices – you can really push it.

There are so many ways to approach cooking meat too – countless flavours, textures and cooking methods, depending on whether you're aiming for poached and soft, seared and caramelised, puffed up with crunchy crackling, or slow-cooked and tender...

You need to start with the butchery. Get to know the cuts you like and, above all, get to know your butcher – that's the best way of ensuring quality. Great local butchers, whether they ply their trade in shops or in farmers' markets, are fantastic sources of ideas for how best to cook your meat.

On the Sundays Beth and I manage to spend at home, hanging out with the dogs, or with a few mates round for a beer or two, we like to have simple, slow-cooked dishes that don't need a lot of fuss to make them taste brilliant: tasty, forgiving cuts, such as beef brisket or short ribs. The Leg of lamb with bay leaves, juniper and thyme, and the Slow-roast harissa lamb are a couple of particular favourites. Lamb, because of its high fat content, is great at taking on strong flavours and slow cooking gives it an amazingly tender and succulent texture – just the thing for a lazy day at home.

Of course, it's not all about the big cuts and the grand dishes. I love the simple Barnsley chop with cumin and coriander – it's something you can rustle up for a quick but substantial weeknight supper. And fairly humble dishes, like Mum's sausage roast, Real ham hamburgers or Cottage pie are some of the most satisfying comfort food you can imagine.

Lemon pepper chicken is one of those retro dishes that withstands the test of time simply because it tastes so good. This recipe makes an easy, tasty midweek tea when it's served with a green pepper salsa.

Lemon pepper chicken with green pepper salsa

SERVES 4

Finely grated zest and
  juice of 2 lemons
4 tablespoons runny honey
3 garlic cloves, grated
2 tablespoons Dijon mustard
4 teaspoons cracked
  black pepper
4 skinless chicken
  supremes, on the bone
4–5 rosemary sprigs
1 lemon, cut into thin slices
700g baby new potatoes

For the salsa
100ml olive oil
4 green peppers, cored
  and cut into 3–4mm dice
1 onion, finely diced
4 tablespoons peeled and
  freshly grated horseradish
2 green chillies, finely sliced
  – seeds and all
2 tablespoons
  marjoram leaves
Salt and freshly ground
  black pepper

To serve
Small handful of flat-leaf
  parsley, finely chopped

In a bowl, mix together the lemon zest and juice, honey, garlic, mustard and black pepper. With a sharp knife, score the chicken 3 or 4 times and rub the marinade into the flesh. Make sure you get it into the cracks. Put the chicken into a bowl with the remaining marinade, stir to coat, cover and refrigerate for up to 2 hours.
.....
When you're ready to cook the chicken, preheat the oven to 200°C/Gas Mark 6. Mix together the rosemary and lemon slices in the bottom of a roasting tin, like a messy carpet. Put the potatoes on top and settle the chicken with its marinade over the top. Roast for 30–35 minutes, until the potatoes and chicken are cooked through. Remove from the oven, cover with tin foil and rest for 10–15 minutes.
.....
While the chicken is cooking, make the salsa. Warm the olive oil in a large frying pan over a medium heat. Add the green peppers and onion, turn the heat up to high and toss them around. When they just start to soften, add the horseradish and chillies. Remove from the heat, stir in the marjoram and season to taste.
.....
Either spoon the salsa over the tray of chicken and potatoes and scatter with the chopped parsley before serving, or serve the salsa on the side.

This is really a bit of a cheat as you're not so much cooking a stew as just heating things up. It's easy to do and tastes really good – a great one-pot dinner for a cosy evening in. I love the smoked flavour and in this recipe, it infuses everything! If you can't find a whole, smoked chicken at your local butcher or shop, there are some great mail order places online.

Smoked chicken stew

SERVES 2-4

1 smoked chicken, about 1.5kg
100g smoked lardons
1 tablespoon thyme leaves, stalks reserved
About 400ml Rich chicken stock (see p. 285)
100g baby new potatoes
100g baby turnips
100g baby onions, peeled
100g baby carrots
100g baby sweetcorn
100g French beans
50g butter
2 tablespoons crème fraîche
Small handful of finely chopped flat-leaf parsley

Joint the chicken into 8 pieces – the breasts, wings, drumsticks and thighs. Put the carcass and any trimmings to one side.

.....

Warm a large casserole over a medium heat and add the lardons. Sweat them gently in their rendered fat. When they start to brown, remove them from the pan with a slotted spoon and drain them on kitchen paper. Pour away the fat and add the smoked chicken carcass to the casserole along with the thyme stalks and chicken stock and bring to the boil. Turn the heat down and simmer for 10–15 minutes on a low heat to infuse the stock with the smoky flavour.

.....

Strain the stock into a bowl through a fine sieve, discard the carcass and thyme stalks, then return the liquid to the casserole. Put the casserole on a medium heat, add the potatoes, turnips and onions to the stock and cook for 5–8 minutes.

.....

Add the chicken pieces and the carrots. Gently poach for a further 5 minutes. Add the sweetcorn, beans and lardons and bring to the boil. Stir in the butter and crème fraîche and bring back to the boil. Cook for 1–2 minutes until the liquid is thickened slightly and the vegetables are cooked. Stir in the thyme leaves and parsley and serve immediately.

Who doesn't love chicken Kiev? I think it's the best thing ever! The Burnt onion ketchup on page 16 would be a great accompaniment.

Classic chicken Kiev

SERVES 2

100g softened butter
3 tablespoons finely
   chopped flat-leaf parsley
2 garlic cloves, grated
1 teaspoon salt
½ teaspoon cayenne pepper
2 large skinless
   chicken breasts
150g plain flour
2 large eggs, beaten
150g fine panko breadcrumbs
Vegetable, groundnut or
   other flavourless oil,
   for cooking
Flaky sea salt
Crisp green salad, to serve

In a bowl, beat together the butter, parsley, garlic, salt and cayenne pepper with a wooden spoon. Set aside but don't refrigerate as the butter must remain soft.

· · · · ·

Take the chicken breasts and using a sharp, thin knife, make a small hole at the fattest end, then push the knife into the middle of the breast, trying not to cut all of the way through. Keep working the knife around to form a large enough opening to get the butter in. With a small spoon, fill each of the chicken breasts with as much butter as you can get in the hole.

· · · · ·

Dust the breasts all over with the flour, then dip them into the beaten eggs. Finally, roll them around in the panko breadcrumbs. Place the chicken on a plate, cover and refrigerate for at least 20 minutes or until needed.

· · · · ·

Preheat the oven to 200°C/Gas Mark 6. Warm a little oil in a large, non-stick frying pan over a low–medium heat. Place the Kievs in the pan and colour gently for 3–4 minutes on each side. When the chicken breasts have taken on a lovely golden colour, sprinkle them with a pinch of flaky sea salt, place on an oven tray and roast for 10–15 minutes until they are cooked through. Serve with a crisp green salad.

This is a fantastic roast chicken recipe. Brining the bird first makes for an exceptionally tender roast, so it's definitely worth the small amount of effort it takes. The meaty king oyster mushrooms and rustic earthiness of the Jerusalem artichokes give the finished dish a great depth of flavour.

Mushroom butter chicken with Jerusalem artichokes

SERVES 4

1 large chicken, about 1.8kg
1 quantity of Brine (see p. 143)
225g softened butter
40g mixed dried mushrooms, blitzed to a powder in a spice grinder or cleaned coffee grinder
2 tablespoons finely chopped shallots (about 1 shallot)
2 teaspoons thyme leaves
1 garlic clove, grated
1 teaspoon salt
Finely grated zest and juice of 1 lemon, plus an extra good squeeze for the artichokes
Vegetable oil, for greasing your hands and for cooking
500g Jerusalem artichokes
6–8 king oyster mushrooms, cut in half lengthways
400ml Rich chicken stock (see p. 285)
100g toasted hazelnuts
2 tablespoons finely chopped sage
Salt and freshly ground black pepper

To serve (optional)
Chicken gravy (see p. 285)

Place the chicken in a large container, pour over the brine, cover and leave it in the fridge for 8 hours. Remove from the brine and pat dry with kitchen paper.
.....

In a mixing bowl, beat together 150g of the butter, the mushroom powder, shallots, thyme, garlic and salt. Sprinkle the lemon zest over the top and mix into the butter.
.....

Lightly oil your hands and gently prise the chicken skin away from the breasts, pushing your fingers between the skin and the flesh, but being careful not to tear it. Rub the soft butter underneath the skin with your hands, trying to spread it all over. If you like, you can now put the chicken into the fridge for 1–2 days before you cook it.
.....

Preheat the oven to 220°C/Gas Mark 7.
.....

Place the chicken on an ovenproof rack inside a roasting tin, season and roast for 1 hour until cooked. It may need a little longer, but not much – an instant-read thermometer should read 70°C. Remove from the oven, baste with the buttery tin juices and leave to rest, covered in tin foil, for 25 minutes.
.....

While the chicken is resting, prepare the Jerusalem artichokes. Peel them and halve 400g of them, then drop these into a bowl of water to which you've added a good squeeze of lemon juice so they don't go brown. Use a mandolin to slice the remaining 100g very thinly and put these in the water too.
.....

Continues overleaf

Mushroom butter chicken with Jerusalem artichokes

Continued

Heat a large frying pan over a medium heat and drizzle in a
little oil. Place the mushrooms in the pan, cut-side down, and fry
until they are golden brown. Turn them over and pour in 50ml
of the chicken stock and simmer to reduce to a glaze. When the
mushrooms are cooked, remove them from the pan and reserve.
.....

Wipe out the frying pan and drizzle in a little more oil and the
remaining 75g of butter. Warm over a medium heat then add
the halved Jerusalem artichokes and fry, tossing them around
in the hot fat for 4–5 minutes. Pour in the remaining chicken
stock and bring to the boil. Simmer to reduce the stock until
thickened slightly.
.....

When the artichokes are soft, return the mushrooms to the pan,
add the lemon juice and season with salt and pepper. Stir in the
hazelnuts and sage, then the thinly sliced artichokes. Serve
immediately, with the chicken and a jug of the warm chicken
gravy on the side, if using.

This is my version of a French classic – chicken roasted with forty cloves of garlic. With this recipe – and all my recipes – I'm trying to get as much flavour as possible out of every ingredient, which is why I use the lovely, garlicky oil used to cook the chicken to make the mayonnaise.

Forty-cloves-of-garlic brined chicken

SERVES 4

1 large chicken, about 1.8kg
100ml chicken stock
100ml white wine
2 tablespoons brandy
1 medium potato, peeled
4 bay leaves
250ml extra virgin olive oil
1 tablespoon flaky sea salt
1 tablespoon cracked
  black pepper
40 garlic cloves,
  separated but not peeled
1 small bunch of thyme
Vegetable oil,
  for pan-roasting

For the brine
2 litres water
400g flaky sea salt
390g demerara sugar
2 tablespoons black
  peppercorns
4 cloves
2 bay leaves
2 thyme sprigs

To make the brine, bring all of the ingredients to the boil in a large saucepan, stirring to make sure that the sugar and salt dissolve. Leave to cool to room temperature then chill in the fridge. When chilled, place the chicken in the brine, cover and leave in the fridge for 8 hours. Remove the chicken and pat dry on kitchen paper.

......

Preheat the oven to 210°C/Gas Mark 7.

......

Pour the chicken stock, white wine and brandy into a large casserole and bring to the boil over a medium–high heat. Add the potato and bay leaves. Place the chicken in the casserole and pour in the olive oil. Season with the flaky sea salt and black pepper, then throw in the 40 garlic cloves and the thyme. Put a lid on the casserole and place in the oven for 45–60 minutes, until the chicken is cooked. Test the thickest part of the thigh meat with an instant-read thermometer – it should have an internal temperature of 70°C.

......

Remove the chicken from the casserole and put it into a roasting tin. Turn the oven down to 60°C/Gas Mark ¼ and place the chicken in the oven to rest.

......

Place a fine sieve over a jug and drain the cooking liquor into it. Carefully lift the whole potato out, place it on a small plate and put it into the fridge to chill. Gently pour off the cooking oil from the jug – it will have separated and floated to the top. Keep this oil as you are going to make the mayonnaise with it. Place a frozen freezer block or a plastic bag filled with ice cubes into the oil to cool it down quickly. Also, reserve the cooking liquid beneath the oil.

......

Continues overleaf

Forty-cloves-of-garlic brined chicken
Continued

For the mayonnaise
2 tablespoons Dijon mustard
2 egg yolks
2 tablespoons white
    wine vinegar
Juice of ½ lemon
Salt and freshly ground
    black pepper

Pat the garlic cloves dry on some kitchen paper. Warm a large, non-stick frying pan on a medium heat and drizzle in a little vegetable oil. Add the garlic cloves and roast them in the pan until they are browned and toasted – be careful not to burn them. They will already be soft inside.
. . . . .

Pour the remaining cooking liquor that was underneath the cooking oil into a saucepan and simmer it to reduce it to a glaze. Remove the chicken from the oven and blowtorch it to get a dark, even colour. Pour over the reduced glaze.
. . . . .

To make the mayonnaise, place the chilled potato, mustard, egg yolks and vinegar in a food processor and purée until smooth. With the motor running, slowly pour the chilled cooking oil through the feed tube, until it emulsifies into a thick mayonnaise. Add the lemon juice and season with salt and black pepper.
. . . . .

To serve, carve the chicken into 10 pieces – breasts, wings, wing tips, drumsticks and thighs. Transfer to a serving platter and serve with the roasted garlic cloves and the mayonnaise.

For me this is the ultimate Saturday-night chicken dish. A little spicy, nutty and naughty! Be careful – it needs to be cooked slowly or it can burn, so be patient and you will be rewarded. Start planning this dish on a Thursday for the best Saturday tea ever. If you're in more of a hurry, it's fine to skip the brining part of the recipe.

Whole satay chicken

SERVES 4

1 large chicken, about 1.8kg
1 quantity of Brine
   (see p. 143; optional)
1 tablespoon ground turmeric
1 tablespoon ground cumin
400g blanched,
   unsalted peanuts
3 garlic cloves, grated
2 lemongrass sticks,
   finely chopped
5cm piece of galangal,
   peeled and grated
1 x 400ml tin coconut milk
60ml ketjap manis
   (Indonesian sweet soy
   sauce) or 40ml dark
   soy sauce mixed with
   20g dark muscovado sugar
2 tablespoons chilli flakes
Finely grated zest of 1 lime

⌄

If you're brining the chicken, place it in the brine, cover and refrigerate for 8 hours. Remove and pat dry.
.....
Mix together the turmeric, cumin and enough water to make a paste and rub it into the chicken. Wrap in cling film and put it in the fridge overnight.
.....
Meanwhile, roast the peanuts for the satay sauce and the salad. Preheat the oven to 180°C/Gas Mark 4. Scatter the peanuts on a large oven tray. Roast until they are golden brown; this should take 8–10 minutes. Remove them from the oven and leave to cool completely.
.....
When cold, set aside 150g of the roasted peanuts for the salad. Put the rest in a food processor and pulse briefly – there should be a mixture of fine and coarse pieces.
.....
In a pestle and mortar or a clean food processor, pound or whizz the garlic, lemongrass and galangal into a fine paste. Transfer to a bowl and mix in the coconut milk, ketjap manis (or soy-muscovado mixture), chilli flakes, lime zest and chopped peanuts. At this point, you can refrigerate the satay marinade until needed.
.....
The next day, preheat the oven to 120°C/Gas Mark ½. Place the chicken in a roasting tin and pour over all of the marinade. Roast for 2 hours, basting halfway through.
.....
Continues overleaf

Whole satay chicken
Continued

For the sour chilli dip
2 red peppers, cored, deseeded
   and roughly chopped
4 red chillies, stems
   removed, roughly
   chopped – seeds and all
3 garlic cloves, grated
100ml white wine vinegar
75g caster sugar
1 tablespoon cornflour mixed
   with 2 teaspoons water
Juice of 2 limes
1 teaspoon chilli flakes
   (add an extra ½ teaspoon
   if you like it very hot)
Pinch of salt

For the salad
2 bunches of spring onions,
   cut on the diagonal into
   2cm lengths
1 bunch of coriander,
   leaves picked off,
   stems finely chopped
½ cucumber, thinly sliced
1–2 green chillies, thinly
   sliced – seeds and all
4 tablespoons dark soy sauce
3 tablespoons sesame oil
2 tablespoons runny honey
Juice of 2 limes

After 2 hours, turn the oven up to 200°C/Gas Mark 6 and continue to cook for a further 20 minutes. Be careful that the oven isn't too hot and watch that the chicken doesn't burn. If you need to, add a splash or two of water to the roasting tin if it looks like it's going to burn. Remove and leave to rest for 20 minutes, basting the chicken in the satay sauce while it rests.

· · · · ·

While the chicken is resting, make the sour chilli dip. Place the red peppers, chillies, garlic, vinegar and sugar in a food processor and blend to a rough purée. Pour this mixture into a saucepan, bring to the boil and simmer for about 3 minutes. Whisk in the cornflour mixture and cook until it thickens; it should take a couple of minutes. Finish with the lime juice, chilli flakes and salt. Leave to cool.

· · · · ·

To make the salad, first roughly chop the reserved roasted peanuts. Place them in a bowl with the spring onions, coriander leaves and stems, cucumber and chillies. In a small bowl, whisk together the soy sauce, sesame oil, honey and lime juice. Pour this over the salad and mix thoroughly. Serve with the chicken and chilli sauce.

A pineapple glaze not only brings super sweetness to a dish, but it's also highly acidic so using it as a marinade tenderises the meat, making it really succulent. I use chicken here, but this recipe works brilliantly with pork ribs as well. Don't be put off by the long list of ingredients: the barbecue sauce will last for three weeks in the fridge and the seasoning mixture keeps for months, so it will see you all the way through the barbecue season.

Barbecued pineapple chicken

SERVES 2–4

1 large chicken, backbone cut out and spatchcocked (ask your butcher to do this for you if you like)

For the barbecue seasoning
70g dark muscovado sugar
2 tablespoons flaky sea salt
2 tablespoons ground coriander
2 tablespoons dried thyme
2 tablespoons cracked black pepper
2 teaspoons garlic powder
2 teaspoons onion powder
2 teaspoons ground allspice
2 teaspoons ground cinnamon
2 teaspoons chilli powder
1 teaspoon cayenne pepper

For the barbecue sauce
600ml pineapple juice
2–3 hot red chillies, finely chopped – seeds and all
6cm piece of fresh ginger, peeled and finely grated
400ml tomato ketchup
90ml red wine vinegar
90ml Worcestershire sauce
4 tablespoons dark muscovado sugar
3 tablespoons dark soy sauce
2 teaspoons salt
2 teaspoons cayenne pepper

First, make the barbecue seasoning. Mix all of the ingredients together and keep in an airtight container until needed. It will keep for up to 3 months.
. . . . .
Next, make the barbecue sauce. Pour the pineapple juice into a saucepan, add the chillies and ginger and boil until reduced by half. Add the ketchup, vinegar, Worcestershire sauce, sugar and soy sauce and continue to reduce until it thickens and has a rich, glossy texture. Remove from the heat and season with the salt and cayenne pepper. This sauce will keep sealed in the fridge for up to 3 weeks.
. . . . .
Mix all of the ingredients for the marinade together with 200ml of the barbecue sauce. Place the spatchcocked chicken in a large bowl and pour the marinade over the top. Cover with cling film and refrigerate for 24 hours.
. . . . .
The next day, heat the barbecue. If you are using a two-tiered gas barbecue, have the temperature set to 150°C; try to regulate the temperature on a charcoal barbecue so it's moderate and constant.
. . . . .
Place some woodchips in the bottom of a large roasting tray and put a grill rack on top. Feed two skewers through the thickest part of the chicken in a cross shape to keep it firm and make it easier to handle.
. . . . .
Put the chicken on top of the rack, skin-side up, and cook in the barbecue, with the lid down. Cook for 1–1½ hours, basting with the marinade about 3–4 times during the cooking process. The chicken will take on a lovely, sticky glaze.
. . . . .
Continues overleaf

Barbecued pineapple chicken
Continued

For the pineapple marinade
300ml pineapple juice
100ml red wine vinegar
6 tablespoons
  barbecue seasoning
3 tablespoons dark
  muscovado sugar
1 teaspoon cracked
  black pepper

For the pineapple salsa
1 medium pineapple,
  cored and finely diced
1 red chilli, halved,
  deseeded and finely diced
1 green chilli, halved,
  deseeded and finely diced
1 red onion, finely diced
Juice of 1 lime
Small handful of coriander
  leaves, finely chopped

To serve
Bunch of coriander leaves,
  roughly chopped
Lime wedges

Alternatively, you could roast the chicken in an oven set at 200°C/Gas Mark 6 for approximately 40–45 minutes, depending on the size of the chicken. Whichever method you choose, it's done when an instant-read thermometer stuck into the fleshiest part reads 70°C. Remove from the barbecue or oven and rest for 15 minutes.

·····

While the chicken is resting, toss together all of the ingredients for the salsa.

·····

Serve the chicken sprinkled with the coriander, with some of the salsa and lime wedges on the side.

Malty and sticky, these guys are great for a barbecue, picnic or party. If you have any left over, they're perfect cold the next day for lunch or flaked and mixed with mayonnaise as a tasty filling for a sandwich.

Sticky drumsticks

SERVES 4

12 chicken drumsticks
2 garlic cloves, grated
3cm piece of ginger,
  peeled and grated
2 tablespoons sesame oil
3 tablespoons sesame
  seeds, toasted lightly
  in a dry frying pan
1 bunch of spring onions,
  trimmed and finely sliced
1 green chilli, finely sliced –
  seeds and all

For the marinade
160g runny honey
160ml dark soy sauce
300ml chicken stock
120g malt extract

To make the marinade, pour the honey into a small stainless steel saucepan (it helps if the pan has a light interior rather than a dark one, as it's easier to judge the colour of the honey as it caramelises) and warm on a medium–high heat. Cook the honey until it starts to turn a deep, rich shade of amber, then pour in the soy sauce and chicken stock to stop it cooking further. Bring to the boil and whisk in the malt extract. Remove from the heat and cool.

. . . . .

Place the drumsticks in a bowl and pour over the marinade. Mix in the garlic and ginger, cover the bowl with cling film and leave to marinate in the fridge for at least 2 hours; overnight is even better.

. . . . .

Preheat the oven to 170°C/Gas Mark 3.

. . . . .

Put the drumsticks in a roasting tin with their marinade. Cook for 45–50 minutes, basting 3–4 times during the cooking, until the chicken is cooked through and the meat comes away from the bone easily. The drumsticks should be glossy and sticky.

. . . . .

Remove the tray from the oven and immediately drizzle with the sesame oil and toss in the sesame seeds. Throw in the spring onions and the chilli. Roll the drumsticks around, making sure that they are all evenly coated. Serve hot or cold.

This pie looks impressive but it's actually very easy to make and tastes fantastic. I've made it with chicken here, but you can try pork or beef if you fancy – it will taste just as good.

Chicken, bacon & pistachio pie

SERVES 4

Vegetable oil, for cooking
250g smoked or unsmoked bacon, diced
400g minced chicken, leg meat only if at all possible (you could ask your butcher to do this for you)
2 onions, finely diced
2 garlic cloves, grated
200g button mushrooms, sliced
500ml Rich chicken stock (see p. 285)
1 tablespoon brined green peppercorns, drained
100g shelled pistachio nuts, roughly chopped
2 tablespoons chopped oregano
1 x 250g packet of filo pastry
150g butter, melted
2 tablespoons dried oregano
Salt and freshly ground black pepper

Warm a saucepan over a medium heat and drizzle in a little oil. Add the bacon and cook until it starts to brown. Add the minced chicken and cook, stirring now and again, until it has turned golden brown.

.....

Place a colander over a bowl and drain the meat, reserving the fat. Pour the fat back into the pan and put it back on the hob over a medium–low heat. Add the onion and garlic and cook for about 10 minutes, stirring occasionally, until soft. Tip in the mushrooms and the cooked mince. Cover with the chicken stock and bring to the boil. Turn the heat down to a simmer and cook until the sauce reduces and thickens – about 10–15 minutes. Turn off the heat and stir in the green peppercorns and most of the chopped pistachios, saving some for garnishing later. Add the fresh oregano and season. Leave to cool.

.....

Take a sheet of filo pastry and brush it with the melted butter, sprinkle on some dried oregano and place a second piece of filo directly on top of the first. Brush that sheet of filo with butter and sprinkle with dried oregano too. Repeat the process until you have 6 or 7 layers – work quickly so the filo doesn't dry out.

.....

Preheat the oven to 200°C/Gas Mark 6. Grease a 20cm-diameter cast-iron dish or heavy, ovenproof frying pan with some of the melted butter and then press in the layered filo. Spoon in the chicken mixture, pushing it right up to the edges. Bring the edges of the filo up over the top of the filling.

.....

Take another sheet of filo, brush it with butter and sprinkle on a little dried oregano, then push it down on top of the filling. Repeat with another 5 layers, but place them on top of each other with a few creases to add a little texture. Brush the top layer with butter and sprinkle on the remaining pistachios. Bake for 12–15 minutes, until the top is crisp and golden and the middle is hot. Serve straight away.

As pie fillings go, ham and mushroom is, without a doubt, one of the world's greatest. I've made this classic even more special here by adding dried mushroom powder to the pastry.

160g butter
400g chestnut mushrooms, stalks removed
Vegetable oil, for cooking
1 onion, diced
60g plain flour
250ml Ham stock (see p. 286)
150ml double cream
200ml milk
2 tablespoons Dijon mustard
2 tablespoons white wine
500g ham, cut into large dice
2 tablespoons thyme leaves

For the pastry
600g plain flour, plus a little more for dusting
100g mixed dried mushrooms, blitzed to a powder in a spice grinder or cleaned coffee grinder
400g butter, chilled and cut into small cubes
2 large eggs, lightly beaten
2–6 tablespoons iced water
Vegetable oil, for greasing the pie dish

Classic ham & mushroom pie

To make the pastry, in a stand mixer with the beater attachment combine the flour and dried mushroom powder. Add the butter and mix slowly until it has the consistency of breadcrumbs. Add the eggs and 2 tablespoons of the iced water. Bring together to form a dough. You may need to add a little more water. Once the pastry has come together, remove it from the bowl and work it together gently with your hands until it forms a smooth pastry. Wrap in cling film and leave in the fridge to rest for at least 1 hour, and up to a day.
∙∙∙∙∙

To make the filling, melt 100g of the butter in a large frying pan over a high heat. When the butter is foaming, add the mushrooms and fry very quickly until coloured. Drain and set aside in a bowl.
∙∙∙∙∙

Warm the mushroom frying pan on a medium–low heat – don't bother to clean it first – and drizzle in a little oil. Add the onion and sweat gently for about 15 minutes, stirring from time to time, until soft. Add the onions to the bowl of mushrooms.
∙∙∙∙∙

In a saucepan over a medium–low heat, melt the remaining 60g of butter. Add the flour and cook, stirring, for a couple of minutes. Add the stock, cream and milk. When thick, cook for a further 4–5 minutes, stirring. Add the mustard and white wine, turn off the heat and leave to cool a little.
∙∙∙∙∙

Add the ham and thyme to the mushroom and onion mixture, then stir this into the white sauce. Transfer to a bowl, cover with cling film and chill in the fridge for a couple of hours.
∙∙∙∙∙

To glaze the pie
2 egg yolks
2 tablespoons double cream
2 tablespoons thyme leaves
2 teaspoons flaky sea salt

Preheat the oven to 190°C/Gas Mark 5. Divide the pastry into two pieces, the larger one being two thirds of the whole. Take the larger piece and, on a surface lightly dusted with flour, roll it out into a circle big enough to line a 22cm pie dish. Brush the pie dish with a little oil and push the rolled-out pastry into the dish. Pour in the chilled pie filling, pushing it right into the edges.

· · · · ·

Roll out the remaining pastry into a circle large enough to form the lid and use a cutter to make a small hole in the middle (this will let the air escape while the pie is cooking). Use a rolling pin to pick up the pastry, then drape it over the top of the pie. Crimp the edges together with your finger and thumb and cut away any excess pastry.

· · · · ·

To glaze the pie, mix together the egg yolks and double cream and brush on top of the pie, then sprinkle over the thyme leaves and flaky sea salt.

· · · · ·

Place the pie on a baking tray and cook for 40–50 minutes until the pastry is crisp and golden. If it starts to colour too early, you can cover the top with a layer of tin foil. Remove from the oven and leave to rest for 10–15 minutes before serving.

Photographs overleaf

I don't know if there's anything more cosy than a meatloaf dinner, served with lots of gravy. This is my version of the American classic, spiced up and served with onion rings flecked with green chilli. Meatloaf is great hot or cold and it'll keep in the fridge for two to three days. It's perfect with a bit of salad for lunch, or even between two slices of soft white bread with some ketchup for a killer sandwich.

Meatloaf with pickled onion rings

SERVES 6

600g minced beef
600g minced pork belly
  (ask your butcher to
  mince it for you if you like)
100g minced bacon
  (ask your butcher to
  mince it for you if you like)
3 garlic cloves, grated
1 tablespoon salt
2 teaspoons fennel seeds
2 teaspoons chilli flakes
50g butter
3 onions, diced
75g fresh breadcrumbs
1 egg, lightly beaten
2 teaspoons Tabasco sauce
2 teaspoons Worcestershire
  sauce
1 tablespoon creamed
  horseradish
2 tablespoons finely
  chopped sage
2 tablespoons finely
  chopped flat-leaf parsley
1 tablespoon thyme leaves
Salt

Put the minced meats in a large mixing bowl with the garlic, salt, fennel seeds and chilli flakes. Work the mixture together with your hands, kneading it like you would bread, until it's well combined and stiffens up a bit. Cover with cling film and refrigerate overnight.

When you're ready to make the meatloaf, melt the butter in a saucepan over a medium heat, add the onion and a pinch of salt and cook gently for about 15 minutes, stirring from time to time, until soft and translucent. Leave to cool.

Put the cooled onion into the mixing bowl with the meat. Add the breadcrumbs, egg, Tabasco sauce, Worcestershire sauce, horseradish, sage, parsley and thyme. Mix everything together with your hands until well combined.

Line the bottom and sides of a 900g loaf tin with baking parchment – let some hang over the sides as this will make it easier to lift the meatloaf out of the tin later. Add the meat, pushing it right into the corners and trying to eliminate any air gaps. Smooth the top down with the back of a wet spoon. Leave to rest in the fridge for 1 hour.

Preheat the oven to 160°C/Gas Mark 3. Place the meatloaf tin on a baking tray and bake for 1 hour. (If you want to serve the meatloaf warm, start making the onion rings when it's in the oven.) When the meatloaf starts to form a light crust on top, take it out of the oven. Mix all the glaze ingredients together and brush them over the top of the loaf. Put it back into the oven to cook for a further 10–15 minutes, until it's glazed and a dark golden brown. Remove from the oven and leave to cool a bit while you finish the recipe.

Continues overleaf

Meatloaf with pickled onion rings
Continued

For the meatloaf glaze
70g tomato ketchup
2 teaspoons creamed
   horseradish
1 teaspoon Tabasco sauce
1 teaspoon
   Worcestershire sauce
½ teaspoon salt
½ teaspoon ground
   white pepper

For the pickled onion rings
4 large onions, cut into
   rings about 1cm thick
150ml Pickle liquor
   (see p. 291)
125g plain flour, plus a
   little more for dusting
10g fresh yeast, crumbled
250ml milk, at body
   temperature
Vegetable oil, for deep-frying
2 green chillies, finely
   chopped – seeds and all
Salt

To serve
Chicken gravy (see p. 285)

To make the onion rings, place the rings in a bowl and pour over the pickle liquor. Leave to steep for 25–30 minutes. Meanwhile, make the batter by mixing the flour and yeast together, then whisk in the milk. Leave the batter to stand for 30–40 minutes in a warm place.

. . . . .

Preheat the oil in a deep fat fryer to 180°C. Drain the onion rings and dust them in a little flour. Dip them into the batter then fry them until golden brown and crisp – you will need to do this in batches but make sure the oil comes back up to temperature between each batch. Drain the onions on kitchen paper and season with salt and the chillies.

. . . . .

When ready to serve, warm up the chicken gravy. Lift the meatloaf out of the tin using the baking parchment to help you, cut into thick slices and serve with the gravy poured over the top and the onion rings on the side.

If you love pork, you'll love these – black pudding, sausage meat and bacon all rolled into one. If there's a better posh breakfast or brunch dish, I don't know what it is. Serve the pigs in blankets with fried or poached eggs and lots of thick, buttered toast.

Ultimate pigs in blankets

SERVES 4

250g good-quality
   black pudding,
   any casing removed
1 egg
2 tablespoons double cream
2 tablespoons finely
   chopped sage leaves
16 rashers of smoked streaky
   bacon, rind cut off
4 sausages, the best quality
   you can find
Vegetable oil, for cooking

*For the Cumberland
   sauce glaze*
25g butter
2 banana shallots,
   finely diced
300ml ruby port
200g redcurrant jelly
2 teaspoons ground ginger
2 teaspoons English
   mustard powder
Juice and finely grated
   zest of 1 orange
Juice and finely grated
   zest of 1 lemon
2 tablespoons green
   peppercorns in brine,
   drained and rinsed

To serve
Fried or poached eggs
   and hot, buttered toast

Whizz the black pudding in a food processor until smooth then add the egg and cream, and blend to a rich paste. Scrape into a bowl, stir in the sage, cover and refrigerate for up to one day.

· · · · ·

With a sharp knife, carefully stretch out the bacon rashers as if you're going to wrap sausages for pigs in blankets at Christmas. Lay a sheet of cling film on your worktop and line up about four pieces of streaky bacon next to each other to form a rectangle. Spoon a quarter of the blended black pudding on to the bacon at a short end and, with a palette knife, spread it out to cover half the bacon.

· · · · ·

Peel the sausage skin from the sausages but keep them in a sausage shape. Place one on top of the black pudding then carefully roll the black pudding and bacon over the top of the sausage, using the cling film as a guide – a bit like how you might use a sushi mat to wrap up pieces of sushi. Wrap the whole thing in the stretched bacon and roll it up tightly in the cling film. Secure the ends by twisting the cling film and tying it into a knot. Repeat with the 3 remaining sausages. Refrigerate for at least 2 hours, but preferably overnight.

· · · · ·

To make the Cumberland sauce glaze, melt the butter in a saucepan over a medium–low heat, add the shallots and sweat gently for about 10 minutes until soft, stirring from time to time. Add the port and redcurrant jelly, raise the heat and bring to the boil. Turn the heat down to a simmer and cook for 10–15 minutes until the jelly has dissolved and the liquid has reduced a little. Add the ginger and mustard. Pour in the orange and lemon juices and add the zests. Stir, bring back to the boil and simmer until reduced by half. Stir in the green peppercorns and remove from the heat.

· · · · ·

Continues overleaf

Ultimate pigs in blankets

Continued

Preheat the oven to 170°C/Gas Mark 3. Warm a large, non-stick ovenproof frying pan over a medium heat and pour in a little oil. Take the cling film off the black pudding rolls and cook them gently until the bacon takes on an even colour all over. Put the pan in the oven and roast for 8–10 minutes.

·····

Remove the pan from the oven, gently pour away any rendered fat and then put it back on the hob over a medium–high heat. Pour in the Cumberland sauce. Bring to the boil and reduce the sauce to a glaze, while basting the sausages to give them a lovely, rich, glossy shine.

·····

Serve as a very hearty breakfast or brunch with some eggs and hot, buttered toast.

I call this my English breakfast omelette but really it has more in common with a meaty Spanish tortilla. As well as the bacon and black pudding, I've ramped up the spice a bit with chunks of chorizo and green chillies. For me, this is a go-to dish for Sunday brunches and midweek teas.

Full English breakfast omelette

SERVES 2-4

8 new potatoes (about 300g)
2–3 tablespoons vegetable
  or olive oil
100g good-quality black
  pudding, any casing
  removed, cut into
  2cm slices
100g lardons,
  cut into 1cm dice
100g chorizo, the best
  quality you can find
2 banana shallots,
  thinly sliced
2 garlic cloves, grated
1 green chilli, sliced –
  seeds and all
6 eggs, whisked
1 tablespoon finely chopped
  rosemary leaves
1 bunch of flat-leaf parsley,
  leaves only, finely chopped
Salt and freshly ground
  black pepper

Cook the potatoes in boiling, salted water until just soft – about 12–15 minutes. Drain in a colander, leave them to steam and cool, then halve them.

. . . . .

Preheat the oven to 220°C/Gas Mark 7.

. . . . .

Warm a 25cm non-stick ovenproof frying pan over a medium heat and pour in the oil. Fry the black pudding slices on each side until crisp, remove them from the pan and drain on kitchen paper. In the same pan, fry the lardons until they start to brown and the fat renders (runs out into the pan). Add the chorizo and fry with the lardons. The smoky red paprika oil will start to come out of the chorizo. Remove the lardons and chorizo with a slotted spoon and drain on kitchen paper. Once the chorizo is cool enough to handle, slice it thinly.

. . . . .

Add one of the sliced shallots and the garlic to the pan with all of the rendered oil still in it and cook for a few minutes over a medium heat until soft. Add the potatoes and stir so that they take on all of the flavours from the pan. Put the cooked meats back into the pan with the green chilli and stir again.

. . . . .

Reduce the heat under the pan to low. Season the eggs then pour them into the pan. Add the rosemary and half the parsley and stir slowly until the eggs start to firm up. Place the pan in the oven and cook for 5–8 minutes until the eggs have set and are puffed up – almost souffléd. Remove the pan from the oven, sprinkle the remaining shallot and parsley over the top and serve.

Normally made with veal, a schnitzel is a piece of meat bashed out and tenderised then coated in breadcrumbs and fried in butter. An 'executive' fried egg is cooked with all sorts of stuff set into it, in this case pancetta and black pudding, but it could be anything you fancy – chorizo and schnitzel is lovely for soaking up the silky egg yolks.

Pork schnitzel with 'executive' fried duck eggs

SERVES 2

1 pork fillet, about 400g, cut into 2 equal portions
100g plain flour
1 egg, lightly beaten
100g panko breadcrumbs
Vegetable oil, for cooking
75g butter
2 slices of good-quality black pudding, any casing removed
4 thin slices of pancetta
2 duck eggs
Juice of 1 lemon
2 tablespoons brined capers, drained
2 tablespoons finely chopped flat-leaf parsley
Salt and freshly ground black pepper

Place a sheet of cling film on a chopping board and put the two pieces of pork on top. Place a second sheet of cling film on top and bash the pork out using a meat tenderiser or a rolling pin until it's 1.5cm thick. Cover the pork fillets in the flour and shake off any excess. Dip them into the beaten egg then cover them with the panko breadcrumbs.
......

Warm a large frying pan over a medium heat and pour in a little oil. Add 25g of the butter and when it just starts to foam, place the pork schnitzels in the pan and fry gently for about 4–5 minutes until they start to brown. Turn the pork over. Add the black pudding to the pan and cook on each side until crisp. When the schnitzels are browned on both sides, remove them from the pan and season. Drain on a piece of kitchen paper, along with the black pudding.
......

Wipe out the frying pan and, over a medium heat, cook the pancetta slices in their own fat, on both sides, until slightly crisp. Take them out of the pan and place on the kitchen paper with the schnitzels and black pudding and keep warm.
......

Pour a little more oil into the pan and fry the duck eggs on a medium heat. When the whites just begin to set, place a piece of black pudding and the pancetta in the white of each egg and continue to cook so the egg 'sets' around the meat. When the eggs are cooked to your liking, season, place them on top of the schnitzels and pop them on to warmed serving plates.
......

Melt the remaining butter in the frying pan and cook until it's golden. Add the lemon juice, capers and parsley. Spoon this over the eggs and serve immediately.

Pork fillet is a great cut of meat and because there's very little waste it's good value for money. Properly cooked fillet is fantastic, but if you overcook it, the meat can become dry because of its low fat content. To avoid that here, I've topped it with sausage meat and wrapped it in pig's caul to keep it juicy.

Pork fillet patties with bubble & squeak

SERVES 4

2 pork fillets, about 400g each, trimmed of fat and sinew
Vegetable oil, for frying
1 onion, finely diced
1 garlic clove, grated
200g sausage meat
1 teaspoon dried sage
½ teaspoon ground mace
1 teaspoon salt
1 teaspoon cracked black pepper
4 large sage leaves
About 100g pig's caul fat, washed and cut into approximate 15cm squares
Salt and freshly ground black pepper

For the apple and cinnamon relish
2 Braeburn apples, peeled, cored and cut into 5mm dice
1 Granny Smith apple, peeled, cored and cut into 5mm dice
1 onion, finely diced
100ml cider vinegar
75g raisins
75g demerara sugar
1 teaspoon ground cinnamon
1 teaspoon chilli flakes
1 teaspoon salt

Halve the pork fillets, so you have four evenly sized pieces. Place them between two pieces of cling film and with a meat tenderiser or rolling pin, bash them out until they are 1.5–2cm thick and have tenderised a little.

.....

Warm a frying pan over a high heat and drizzle in a little oil. Season the pork fillets and sear one at a time, just until they have taken on some colour on both sides – they should still be raw in the middle. Cool then chill in the fridge.

.....

Add a little more oil to the pan and gently fry the onion and garlic over a medium–low heat for about 10 minutes until soft, stirring from time to time. Cool to room temperature.

.....

Put the cooled onions and garlic, sausage meat, dried sage, mace, salt and black pepper into a mixing bowl and mix to combine. Take the pork fillets out of the fridge and divide the sausage meat evenly into four. Place some sausage mixture on top of a pork fillet, push down and smooth out around the edges then put a sage leaf on top. Lay a piece of caul fat on a chopping board and put the pork fillet on top, sausage-meat-side down. Wrap the fillet in the caul fat, making sure there are no gaps for the sausage meat to escape. You may want to double-wrap it. Once the fillets are all wrapped, pop them on a plate, cover with cling film and refrigerate for 2 hours, or overnight.

.....

Next make the apple and cinnamon relish. Put all the ingredients in a saucepan. Bring to the boil, reduce to a simmer and cook, stirring from time to time, until it has a thin, chutney consistency – this will take 15–20 minutes. Remove from the heat and set aside. The relish can be served hot or cold and will keep for up to 2 weeks sealed in the fridge, so you can make it beforehand if you like.

.....

For the bubble and squeak
600g Desiree potatoes, peeled
   and cut into 2cm dice
300g Brussels sprouts,
   halved – if Brussels
   sprouts aren't in season,
   just use extra cabbage
300g green cabbage,
   tough core removed,
   cut into 2cm dice
2 teaspoons caraway seeds
300g black pudding,
   any casing removed,
   diced (optional)
75g butter, diced

To serve
Meat gravy (see Meat
   stock base, p. 284)

To make the bubble and squeak, put the potatoes into a saucepan and cover with water. Add a good pinch of salt and bring to the boil. Turn the heat down and simmer until the potatoes are just cooked. Drain into a colander in the sink and leave to air dry in their own steam.

Warm a large frying pan over a medium–high heat and drizzle in a little oil. Add the sprouts if you're using them and fry until they're browned around the edges and just beginning to soften. Tip them into a large mixing bowl. Put the pan back on a medium heat and add the cabbage, with a splash of water to help it steam. Season, cover with a lid and cook until just tender.

Put the cabbage in the mixing bowl with the potatoes. Add the caraway seeds and black pudding, if using. With a fork, break up the cooked potato a bit – you still want it to have some texture. While the mixture's still warm, add the butter and season, then mix it all together with your hands. Cover and chill until needed if not cooking straight away.

About an hour before you want to cook the pork, put the fillets on a baking tray and leave them to come to room temperature.

Preheat the oven to 180°C/Gas Mark 4. Roast the pork fillets for 12–15 minutes until browned on the outside and hot in the middle. Remove from the oven and leave to rest for 5 minutes before serving.

To cook the bubble and squeak, pour a little oil into a large frying pan and fry the mixture over a medium heat until browned and warmed through. Serve on warmed plates, with the pork patties and the apple relish, and a jug of the meat gravy to pass around.

Photographs overleaf

Money was short when I was young. My brother and I were growing lads and my mum worked hard to bring us up as best she could as a single parent. We never felt we went without though. Mum would give us rolled sausage meat as a 'roast' instead of an expensive joint, served with all the trimmings. If it's difficult to get your butcher to grind specific cuts for you, simply substitute the shoulder and belly for medium-lean, coarsely ground minced pork.

Mum's sausage roast

SERVES 6-8

1kg pork shoulder, minced
300g pork belly, minced
3 garlic cloves, grated
1 tablespoon salt
1 tablespoon fennel seeds, toasted until fragrant in a dry frying pan, cooled and ground to a powder
2 teaspoons dried oregano
1 teaspoon cayenne pepper
2 dried bay leaves, toasted and ground to a powder
100g dry breadcrumbs
3 tablespoons flat-leaf parsley, finely chopped
1 tablespoon whole fennel seeds, toasted until fragrant in a dry frying pan
1 teaspoon chilli flakes
Finely grated zest of 1 lemon
100ml white wine
50g butter, softened
150ml Pork stock (see p. 286)

To serve
Buttered green cabbage or spring greens or, of course, with all of your favourite vegetable accompaniments for a traditional roast

Place all of the mince in a large mixing bowl. Add the garlic, salt, ground fennel, oregano, cayenne pepper and ground bay leaves. Get your hands in and start to work everything together. You need to knead it like dough for at least 5 minutes. This helps to stretch the proteins and forms a tighter mix that holds its shape better.

.....

Next add the breadcrumbs, parsley, whole fennel seeds, chilli flakes, lemon zest and white wine. Mix together with your hands.

.....

Rub one side of a large sheet of tin foil with the butter. Place the sausage meat on the foil and form into the shape of a log about 25cm long. Try to ensure the meat's quite tightly packed together. Once you have made a giant sausage, roll the tin foil over the top and secure the ends tightly, like a Christmas cracker. Place the roll on a large baking tray and put it into the fridge to firm up for at least 2 hours but preferably overnight.

.....

Preheat the oven to 180°C/Gas Mark 4.

.....

Roast the sausage in its tin foil for 40 minutes. Carefully remove from the oven, unravel the tin foil and put the sausage back in the oven for a further 10–15 minutes, until it's a rich golden brown.

.....

While the sausage is cooking, put the pork stock into a small saucepan and simmer to reduce by half and make a glaze. When you take the cooked sausage out of the oven, glaze it with the reduced pork stock before serving immediately with all your favourite vegetable accompaniments.

Any meat roasted on the bone is brilliant, both for flavour and moistness, but the bone also helps the meat to keep its shape. This great, easy roast is pork's version of a fore rib of beef. Pork and paprika are such good mates – just ask any Hungarian – and this recipe really shows off their friendship. I love to serve this on a cold evening with some mashed potato made with a little smoked butter. Pure pleasure!

Paprika roast rib of pork

SERVES 4

1 x 1.2kg pork rib, on the bone
4 garlic cloves, grated
3 tablespoons smoked paprika
1 teaspoon dried sage
1 teaspoon dried thyme
1 teaspoon dried rosemary
3 tablespoons olive oil
Salt

For the crackling
3 tablespoons white
   wine vinegar
1 tablespoon flaky sea salt

For the pickled white cabbage
Vegetable oil, for cooking
150g garlic sausage, diced
1 large onion, halved and
   very finely sliced
½ white cabbage, tough core
   removed, very finely sliced
100ml white wine
100ml white wine vinegar
20g caster sugar
Cracked black pepper

With a sharp knife, gently remove the skin from the pork rib – you're going to cook this separately in order to get proper crackling. Then carefully cut a slit between the rib bones and the meat, following the contour of the bone. Be careful not to cut all the way through the meat – stop about 2cm from the bottom.

. . . . .

In a small bowl, mix together the garlic, smoked paprika, sage, thyme and rosemary with the olive oil to form a rough paste. Rub most of the mixture into the gap between the bones and meat. Push the meat back on to the bones and tie in between each rib bone securely with kitchen string. Rub the remaining mixture all over the pork. Wrap in cling film and marinate in the fridge overnight. Chill the skin too.

. . . . .

The next day, preheat the oven to 200°C/Gas Mark 6. Place two ovenproof racks in two roasting tins.

. . . . .

Unwrap the pork from the cling film and place it on one of the racks. Season with salt. Place the pork skin on the other rack, skin-side up, and rub in the white wine vinegar then the flaky sea salt. Place both trays in the oven and cook for 35–40 minutes. Keep an eye on the crackling to make sure it doesn't burn.

. . . . .

Using an instant-read thermometer, probe the pork rib at its thickest point. When it reaches 60°C, remove the rib, lightly cover it in tin foil and leave it to rest and finish cooking in its residual heat for 25 minutes. Keep roasting the pork skin until it becomes perfect puffed-up crackling – it will need about 10–20 minutes more, but keep checking it to make sure it doesn't burn. When ready, remove it from the oven and leave to cool.

. . . . .

While the pork is resting, make the pickled cabbage. Warm a
little oil in a large saucepan over a medium heat. Add the garlic
sausage and cook until it starts to brown and crisp up.

.....

Add the onion and sweat gently, stirring from time to time,
until it begins to soften – about 10–15 minutes. Add the cabbage
and give it all a good stir. Pour in the white wine and vinegar and
sprinkle on the sugar. Cook on a medium heat, stirring from time
to time, until most of the liquid evaporates. Season with salt
and cracked black pepper.

.....

Remove the string from the pork and cut it into chops.
Serve on warmed plates, with the crackling and cabbage.

Photographs overleaf

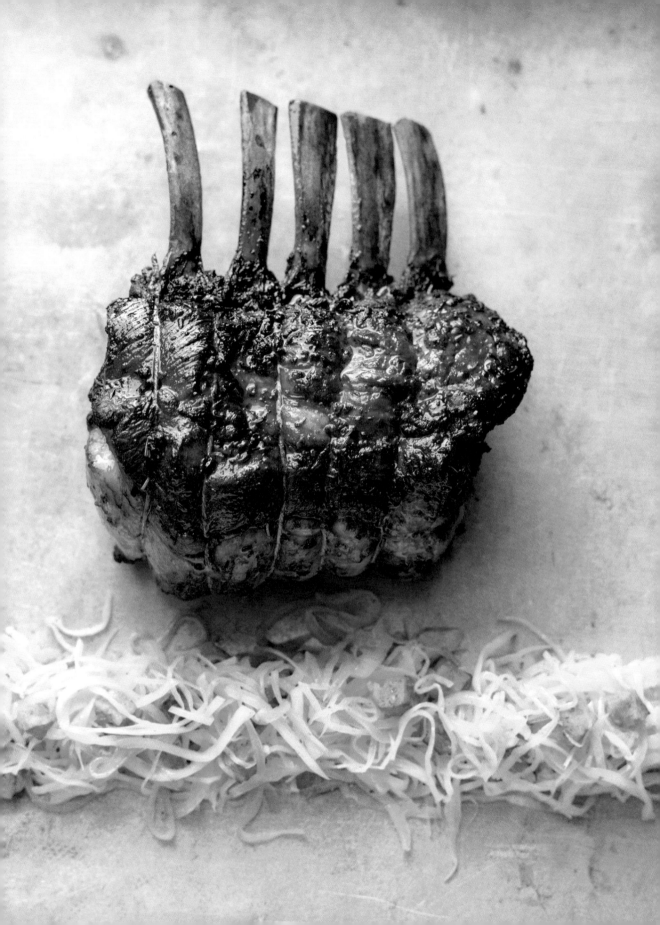

Barbecue food at its best – pork, beer and chillies sounds like a dream dinner to me and this recipe fits the bill. The ribs are cooked slowly to keep the meat tender, then given a quick blast of heat for a sticky, caramelised coating.

Beer-braised spare ribs with pickled cabbage

SERVES 4

2 Bramley apples, with skin
200ml runny honey
100ml malt vinegar
4 tablespoons prepared
  English mustard
4 garlic cloves, grated
3 tablespoons
  Worcestershire sauce
2 tablespoons chilli flakes
1 chicken stock cube,
  crumbled
1 teaspoon salt
1 teaspoon ground
  white pepper
475ml strong, dark ale
1 x 2kg whole rack of
  pork spare ribs

For the pickled cabbage
¼ large, white cabbage,
  tough core removed, finely
  shredded with a mandolin
  or a very sharp knife
1 onion, halved and
  finely sliced
2 tablespoons flaky sea salt
50g palm sugar
2 red chillies, finely
  chopped – seeds and all
2 green chillies, finely
  chopped – seeds and all
200ml Pickle liquor
  (see p. 291)
Handful of coriander,
  leaves only
Handful of mint, leaves only

Grate the unpeeled Bramley apples on the coarse side of a grater. Put into a large, wide mixing bowl with the honey, vinegar, mustard, garlic, Worcestershire sauce, chilli flakes, stock cube, salt and pepper. Stir until well combined then whisk in the beer. Put the pork ribs in the bowl. Try to submerge the meat completely in the marinade. Cover with cling film and refrigerate overnight.

·····

The next day, preheat the oven to 140°C/Gas Mark 1. If you are planning to eat as soon as the ribs are ready, make the pickled cabbage while they are cooking.

·····

Put the pork in a high-sided roasting tin and pour over the marinade. Cover the tray tightly with tin foil, place in the oven and cook for 3 hours, checking halfway through to make sure the marinade hasn't evaporated completely. If you need to, add a splash of water. When they're done, the ribs will be succulent and tender.

·····

At this point, the ribs can either be chilled with their marinade, ready to go into a hot oven or on to a barbecue for caramelising later, or you can simply turn the oven up to 220°C/Gas Mark 8 and cook the pork ribs for 10–15 minutes, until they start to caramelise and glaze.

·····

Put the cabbage into a large mixing bowl with the onion. Sprinkle on the flaky sea salt and mix with your hands. Leave for 25–30 minutes, until the leaves start to wilt and soften.

·····

Put the cabbage and onion in a colander and rinse under cold, running water for a minute or two. Squeeze out excess moisture with a clean tea towel or kitchen paper. Put them in a serving bowl and grate on the palm sugar. Add the chillies, pour on the pickle liquor and leave to steep for 30 minutes. Just before serving, mix in the coriander and mint. Serve with the spare ribs.

Meatballs are always a winner and in this recipe they're cooked in rich ale gravy which gives them quite a punch. I serve them with peas and mousseron mushrooms, which is a fantastic combination as the mushrooms have a woody smell that works beautifully with the sweetness of the peas. If you can't get hold of mousserons, use any well-flavoured and textured mushroom, such as chestnut.

Pork meatballs in brown ale gravy

SERVES 4

Vegetable oil, for cooking
1 onion, finely diced
600g minced pork, the best quality you can find
100g dry breadcrumbs
2 tablespoons prepared English mustard
1½ tablespoons finely chopped rosemary leaves
2 teaspoons dried oregano
2 teaspoons dried sage
2 teaspoons salt
2 teaspoons cracked black pepper
1 egg, lightly beaten
2 tablespoons finely chopped sage

For the gravy
2 shallots, skin on
2 garlic cloves, skin on
4 rosemary sprigs
300ml brown ale
500ml Rich chicken stock (see p. 285)

Warm a splash of oil in a small saucepan over a medium–low heat. Fry the onion, stirring from time to time, until soft – about 10 minutes. Leave to cool.

Place the onion in a large mixing bowl with the pork, breadcrumbs, mustard, rosemary, dried herbs, salt, pepper and egg. Mix thoroughly with your hands. The more you mix it, the better your meatballs will be – you are stretching the proteins and helping to make a firmer ball. Place the mixture in a clean bowl, cover with cling film and pop it in the fridge for at least 1 hour, or overnight.

Divide the pork mixture into four equal portions. Roll six meatballs from each portion so you have 24 meatballs. Put them on a plate, cover with cling film and chill for a further 30 minutes. All of the resting time helps prevent the meatballs from breaking up when you cook them, so it really is worth taking the trouble to do this.

To make the gravy, slice the shallots and garlic, keeping their skins on, and place them in a large saucepan. Add the rosemary sprigs and pour on 250ml of the brown ale. Bring to the boil over a high heat then reduce to a simmer. Cook it down slowly to a glaze, so almost all of the ale is gone and the shallots are soft and brown. Add the chicken stock, turn the heat back up and bring to the boil. Reduce the heat and simmer gently until reduced by a third. Preheat the oven to 190°C/Gas Mark 5.

Continues overleaf

Pork meatballs in brown ale gravy
Continued

For the peas and mushrooms
75g butter
1 onion, finely diced
400g fresh or frozen peas
150ml chicken stock
300g mousseron mushrooms,
    stalks removed, rinsed
    well and drained
4 tablespoons finely
    chopped mint
Salt and freshly ground
    black pepper

Warm a large frying pan over a medium heat and drizzle in a little oil. Gently fry the meatballs in batches, making sure they get a lovely brown colour all over. When browned, remove them from the pan and place them in an ovenproof serving dish.
.....

Pass the gravy through a fine sieve over the top of the meatballs and bake them for 10–12 minutes, until the gravy has thickened a little and the meatballs are cooked through.
.....

While the meatballs are cooking, prepare the peas and mushrooms. Melt the butter in a large saucepan over a medium heat, throw in the onions and cook until soft – about 10–15 minutes, stirring from time to time. Add the peas and pour in the chicken stock. Bring to the boil, season, cook for a couple of minutes then add the mushrooms and turn the heat up to full. Reduce the liquid very quickly, until it is all emulsified with the butter and is like a thicky gravy, and the peas are cooked. Remove from the heat and stir in the mint.
.....

To finish the meatballs, pour in the remaining brown ale and the sage. Give it a good stir and serve with the peas and mushrooms.

Okay, I know practically everyone knows how to make a ragu. It's one of the first things lots of people learn how to cook and one of the easiest things to make, but my version gets an extra, meaty push from roasting the mince to a VERY dark colour first. Also, the long, slow cooking really improves the depth of flavour and if you can leave it, once cooked, until the next day to eat, it improves even more. One of my favourite do-ahead dishes, for sure.

Lasagne

SERVES 6-8

800g minced beef, the best quality you can find
4 star anise
4 cloves
1.4kg ripe plum tomatoes, halved lengthways
20g caster sugar
2 teaspoons flaky sea salt
Vegetable oil, for cooking
200g pancetta, diced
2 Spanish onions, finely diced
2 celery sticks, finely sliced
2 carrots, finely diced
4 garlic cloves, grated
100g demerara sugar
2 tablespoons dried oregano
4 bay leaves
200ml red wine
100ml red wine vinegar
300g button mushrooms, stalks removed, halved
600ml beef stock
4 tablespoons finely chopped oregano
2 tablespoons finely chopped sage
500g fresh lasagne sheets
Salt and freshly ground black pepper

Preheat the oven to 190°C/Gas Mark 5.

.....

Place the mince in a colander and rinse under running water. This sounds like an odd thing to do but it helps break it down and separate it into smaller pieces. Drain and pat dry with kitchen paper.

.....

Put the mince in a roasting tin and roast for 5 minutes. Remove from the oven and stir with a wooden spoon. Tie the star anise and cloves in a muslin bag with kitchen string and add it to the mince. Return the meat to the oven and roast for a further 8–10 minutes; remove, stir again and put it back in the oven. You're trying to get a very dark, even colour all over the mince, as if it's been heavily fried – it will take about 40 minutes. Once it reaches this stage, remove from the oven, tip the meat into a colander and drain the fat. Place the meat and muslin spice bag on one side but do not turn off the oven.

.....

Put the tomatoes on a baking tray. Dust them with the caster sugar and flaky sea salt. Bake for 15–20 minutes until softened. Remove from the oven and place under a hot grill or blast them quickly with a blowtorch to give them a slightly charred taste.

.....

Warm a little oil in a large, heavy-bottomed casserole set over a medium heat. Add the pancetta and cook, stirring from time to time, until it begins to brown. Add the onion, celery, carrots and garlic to the casserole. Cook for 5 minutes until the vegetables begin to soften. Stir in the sugar, dried oregano, bay leaves, red wine and vinegar. Bring to the boil and simmer until reduced by half.

.....

Continues overleaf

Lasagne

Continued

For the white sauce
750ml milk
½ onion
½ bunch of thyme
2 bay leaves
60g butter
60g plain flour
1 teaspoon ground nutmeg
225g freshly grated
    Parmesan cheese

To serve
A crisp green salad
    and crusty bread

Add the minced beef and spice bag, tomatoes, mushrooms and stock to the casserole and bring to the boil. Turn the heat down to a bare simmer and cook gently for 1½ hours, stirring from time to time, until the sauce has thickened and intensified. Stir in the fresh oregano and sage, season and leave to cool. The flavour will improve if the sauce is left overnight in the fridge. Remove the spice bag.

• • • • •

To make the white sauce, pour the milk into a saucepan with the onion, thyme and bay leaves and bring to the boil. Remove from the heat, cover the pan and leave to infuse for 15 minutes.

• • • • •

In a separate pan, melt the butter over a low heat. Add the flour and cook for 2–3 minutes, stirring. Slowly pour the infused milk into the pan through a fine sieve, stirring all the time until you get a thick, glossy sauce. Add the nutmeg and 150g of the Parmesan and stir for a couple of minutes until the cheese has melted. Remove from the heat, stir and season.

• • • • •

Preheat the oven to 190°C/Gas Mark 5.

• • • • •

Get yourself an ovenproof dish, approximately 30 x 20 x 10cm and pour a layer of mince into the bottom. Cover with pasta sheets, a layer of white sauce, a layer of pasta then the ragu again, and so on until you reach the top. Make sure you finish with a layer of white sauce. Sprinkle the remaining Parmesan on top. Bake for 30–45 minutes until warm in the centre and golden brown and bubbling on top.

• • • • •

Serve with a crisp green salad and some crusty bread.

I think this is a fantastic version of a burger. Using gammon puts the 'ham' in the hamburger and helps to season it and give it great depth of flavour. These are really good on a barbecue, or simply cooked for a midweek tea with a big, leafy salad on the side.

Real ham hamburgers

SERVES 4

450g gammon steak, minced
550g boneless short rib
  of beef, fat on, minced
2 teaspoons salt
2 teaspoons dried sage
1 teaspoon cayenne pepper
1 teaspoon garlic powder
1 teaspoon cracked
  black pepper
Vegetable oil, for frying
  (optional)

For the mustard mayonnaise
35g prepared English mustard
1 egg yolk
2 teaspoons white
  wine vinegar
1 tablespoon caster sugar
1 teaspoon fresh lemon juice
310ml vegetable oil
Salt and freshly ground
  black pepper

For the pickled cucumber
1 cucumber
1 tablespoon flaky sea salt
200ml Pickle liquor
  (see p. 291)

For the garnish
200g chestnut mushrooms,
  thinly sliced
Splash of dark soy sauce
150g Comté cheese, grated
4 sourdough buns, sliced in half
8–10 Little Gem lettuce leaves
1 bunch of dill, stalks removed

Put the gammon and beef mince into a mixing bowl and add the salt, sage, cayenne pepper, garlic powder and black pepper; mix together vigorously with your hands. You will feel it stiffen up. Separate into four equal portions. Shape these into burgers, put on a plate, cover in cling film and refrigerate until you need them.
.....

To make the mayonnaise, whisk the mustard, egg yolk, vinegar, sugar and lemon juice in a mixing bowl. Slowly add the oil, whisking continuously, until the mixture emulsifies and thickens. Season.
.....

Slice the cucumber on a slight angle and place in a colander, then scatter over the flaky sea salt. Leave to stand for 10 minutes. Rinse under cold water and pat dry with kitchen paper or a tea towel. Place in a bowl and pour over the pickle liquor. Leave to steep for 1 hour.
.....

Place the chestnut mushrooms in a separate bowl. Season with salt and pepper and a good splash of soy sauce. Leave to cure for 15 minutes – they should have become soft. Wrap the mushrooms in a clean tea towel or some kitchen paper and squeeze out the excess liquid. Roughly chop them.
.....

Fry the burgers on a medium–high heat for about 4–5 minutes per side or place them under a hot grill. When they are just cooked, remove them from the heat, spread the tops with the mushrooms and then cover with the Comté. Place the burgers under a medium–hot grill until the cheese has melted.
.....

Toast the buns. Spread a little mustard mayonnaise on the bottom half of each bun, then top with a couple of Little Gem leaves. Stick a burger on top. Drain a slice of pickled cucumber and put that on the burger, then add a big dollop of the mustard mayonnaise. Cover with a load of dill fronds and the lid of the bun and serve straight away!

This is a great informal lunch dish or a fantastic starter any time. Serve it in the middle of the table – it looks impressive but because you're using bought puff pastry it's very simple to make. Left to go cold, it's a super packed lunch to take to school or the office.

Puff pastry pizza

SERVES 4

200g bavette steak,
   thinly sliced
50g cornflour
About 4 tablespoons
   vegetable oil
Cayenne pepper, to taste
2 teaspoons beef extract
60g Onion jam (see p. 291)
   or use a good-quality
   bought one
Salt and freshly ground
   black pepper

For the base
Plain flour, for dusting
500g all-butter puff pastry,
   defrosted if frozen
1 egg yolk
1 tablespoon double cream

For the sour onions
3 small red onions
100ml cider
100ml cider vinegar
50g demerara sugar

Start with the base. On a lightly floured surface, gently roll out the puff pastry to a circle of approximately 28cm in diameter. Transfer the pastry to a baking sheet lined with baking parchment. Cover with cling film and refrigerate for at least 1 hour, or overnight.

.....

To make the sour onions, start by cutting the peeled onions into sixths lengthways, leaving the root on so the wedges remain intact – they should be about the size and shape of orange segments.

.....

Place the cider, cider vinegar and demerara sugar in a saucepan over a medium heat, stirring to dissolve the sugar. Bring to the boil and add the onion segments. Turn the heat down to a simmer and cook for 5–8 minutes, until the onions start to soften. Turn the onions over and cook for a further 5 minutes until soft. Remove the onions from their cooking liquid and place on a baking tray. Give them a blast with the blowtorch until charred around the edges. If you haven't got a blowtorch, why not?! In that case, stick them under a hot grill instead. Leave to cool.

.....

Preheat the oven to 220°C/Gas Mark 7. Take the pastry out of the fridge and pierce all over with a fork. Mix together the egg yolk and double cream and brush this on top. Bake for 20 minutes, until the pastry rises and is crisp and golden. Turn the oven down to 110°C/Gas Mark ½ and continue to 'dry' the pastry out for a further 15 minutes. Be careful that it doesn't burn!

.....

Continues overleaf

Puff pastry pizza
Continued

For the crème fraîche topping
75g crème fraîche
75g soft blue cheese,
   such as dolcelatte,
   at room temperature
1 tablespoon finely
   chopped chives

To finish
Some fresh watercress

While the pastry's baking, cook the beef. Dust the steak strips in cornflour, shaking off any excess. Heat the oil in a non-stick frying pan over a medium–high heat. Add the steak and fry until crisp; this will take about 6–8 minutes. Don't crowd the pan – you may need to fry the meat in batches to brown it properly. Drain on kitchen paper and season with salt and cayenne pepper while still warm.

· · · · ·

Once the pastry is crisp and dried out, remove from the oven and cool for 5 minutes. Turn the oven back up to 180°C/Gas Mark 4.

· · · · ·

Brush the pizza base with the beef extract. Spread a layer of the onion jam on top, add the beef and return to the oven to warm through for about 5 minutes.

· · · · ·

Put the crème fraîche and blue cheese into a mixing bowl and whisk until thick. Fold in the chives and season – if the mixture's too thick, add a little water to loosen it up.

· · · · ·

Cover the top of the pizza with the charred red onions. Spoon some of the crème fraîche and blue cheese mixture on top, scatter on some watercress and serve.

When I was a kid, my mum used to knock up a great cottage pie and her secret ingredient was a little bit of curry powder. Topped off with cheesy mash and served with buttered peas, it's my ultimate childhood memory. I admit this version is a bit fancier than Mum's; it has two types of cooked beef to give it extra dimension and texture – long-winded, perhaps, but definitely worth the effort.

Cottage pie with blue cheese mash

500g braising steak
50g plain flour
Vegetable oil, for cooking
700ml beef stock
300ml dark ale
2 star anise
1 cinnamon stick
500g minced beef
2 onions, finely diced
2 carrots, finely diced
2 celery sticks, tough strings removed, finely diced
2 tablespoons Curry powder (see p. 290) or use a good-quality bought one
Few splashes of Worcestershire sauce
Salt and freshly ground black pepper

For the mash topping
6 floury potatoes (King Edward or Maris Piper), about 1.2kg, peeled and diced
150ml milk
50g butter
¾ tablespoon prepared English mustard
150g blue cheese (use your favourite), grated
1 teaspoon paprika

To serve
Buttered peas

Preheat the oven to 150°C/Gas Mark 2. Cut the braising steak into 2cm dice, dust in flour and shake off the excess. Warm a large frying pan over a medium–high heat, add a little oil and fry the braising steak until it gets a deep, rich colour all over. Drain the steak on some kitchen paper and transfer to a casserole.

. . . . .

Put the frying pan back on the heat and deglaze it with the stock and ale, scraping up any tasty brown bits from the bottom with a wooden spoon, then pour the liquid over the beef in the casserole. Add the star anise and cinnamon stick and bring to the boil. Put the lid on and braise slowly in the oven for 2½–3 hours, until the beef is tender. Leave to cool.

. . . . .

When cool, remove the cooked steak from the casserole with a slotted spoon and place in a bowl in the fridge until needed. Reserve the remaining cooking liquor.

. . . . .

Wipe out the casserole, then place it over a medium–high heat and pour in a thin layer of vegetable oil. Add the minced beef and cook, stirring constantly, until it's thoroughly browned. The beef shouldn't be grey, you want it to be dry, roasted and crumbly, the colour of the outside of a beef burger; this should take about 10–12 minutes. Drain in a colander to get rid of any fat, and set aside.

. . . . .

Return the casserole to the hob, warm a little more oil over a medium heat, and add the diced vegetables. Cook for 10–12 minutes, stirring from time to time, until they soften. Add the curry powder and stir, making sure the vegetables are thoroughly coated in the spice.

. . . . .

Continues overleaf

Cottage pie with blue cheese mash

Continued

Add the drained minced beef and the reserved braising liquid and bring to the boil. Turn the heat down to a simmer and reduce the stock until it's nice and thick. Add a few splashes of Worcestershire sauce and season. Leave to cool for 20 minutes.

......

When the minced beef has cooled a little, stir in the chilled, braised beef and mix thoroughly, but try not to break up the beef too much. Transfer to a large pie dish or ovenproof serving dish and chill in the fridge for at least 1 hour.

......

Bring a large saucepan of salted water to the boil and cook the potatoes for 14–15 minutes or until soft. Drain in a colander and leave to steam and air dry a little. Meanwhile, warm the milk and butter in a small saucepan. Either put the cooked potato through a potato ricer into a bowl or mash thoroughly with a hand masher. Beat in the hot milk and butter with a wooden spoon to form a semi-firm mashed potato. Mix in the mustard and season.

......

Take the chilled beef mixture from the fridge and pipe the mash on top, or spread it and make little peaks with a fork. Sprinkle the blue cheese on top and dust with the paprika. At this point, you can store the cottage pie covered in cling film in the fridge for up to 2 days if you like.

......

Preheat the oven to 180°C/Gas Mark 4. Put the cottage pie on to a baking tray, stick it in the oven and cook for 20–25 minutes until the middle is very hot. Remove from the oven and place under a hot grill, if needed, just to glaze the blue cheese. Serve immediately with buttered peas.

Beef olives are quite an old-fashioned little dish – parcels of bashed-out steaks, stuffed and then baked – but here I've updated them by stuffing them with spicy minced beef and serving them with crisp circles of fried aubergine seasoned with cumin and cayenne pepper. Ace!

Spiced beef olives with aubergines

SERVES 4

Olive oil, for frying
250g minced beef
75g Milano salami, diced
2 tablespoons cumin seeds
2 teaspoons cracked
    black pepper
150g drained tinned
    kidney beans, rinsed
250ml beef stock
4 x 200g sirloin or
    rump steaks, sinew
    and fat removed
Knob of butter
1 quantity of Tomato sauce
    (see p. 24)
Salt and freshly ground
    black pepper

For the aubergines
2 large aubergines
1 teaspoon cornflour
1 teaspoon plain flour
1 teaspoon ground cumin
1 teaspoon cayenne pepper
1 teaspoon salt
Vegetable oil, for frying
2 tablespoons chopped
    flat-leaf parsley
Lemon wedges, to serve
Green salad, to serve
    (optional)

First, make the beef mince stuffing. Warm a large saucepan over a medium heat and pour in a little olive oil. Add the beef mince and fry, stirring frequently, until the meat has taken on a lovely dark colour and is quite toasted and crispy. Drain the mince in a colander and put the pan back on the heat.

. . . . .

Add a little more oil and fry the diced salami until it starts to crisp up. Stir in the cumin seeds and black pepper then tip the beef back into the pan along with the kidney beans. Pour in the beef stock and bring to the boil. Turn the heat down to a simmer and cook until the stock has reduced and you have a thick, rich mixture. Remove from the heat, place in a clean container, then cover and refrigerate until needed. It will keep quite well in the fridge for a couple of days.

. . . . .

Lay a sheet of cling film on a chopping board and place one of the steaks on top of it. Cover with a second piece of cling film and bash the steak out very thinly with a meat tenderiser or a rolling pin. Repeat this process with the other three steaks. Spoon an equal amount of the spiced beef on to each steak and roll up the steak into a cylinder, overlapping the edges slightly. Secure by tying with kitchen string. Place the rolled and tied beef olives in the fridge to rest for 1–2 hours.

. . . . .

When you're ready to cook the beef olives, place a large, non-stick frying pan over a medium–high heat and drizzle in a little oil. Add the knob of butter and wait until it starts to foam. Season the beef olives and place them in the pan. Cook until nicely coloured all over – this should take 5–8 minutes. Remove and rest on a warm plate.

. . . . .

Continues overleaf

Spiced beef olives with aubergines

Continued

Heat the tomato sauce. Slice the aubergines into 1cm-thick discs. Mix together the cornflour, plain flour, cumin, cayenne pepper and salt. Dust the aubergine slices with the mix.

.....

Warm a large, heavy-bottomed saucepan over a medium heat and pour in a generous splash of oil. Shallow-fry the aubergine slices until golden on both sides and soft in the middle. You will probably have to do this in batches so they crisp – don't crowd the pan otherwise they will stew. Remove and drain on kitchen paper.

.....

Sprinkle the aubergine slices with parsley and black pepper. Remove the string from the beef olives and serve with the tomato sauce, aubergines, lemon wedges and a green salad, if you like.

Short rib is such a lovely cut of beef. It's full of connective tissue that, when slowly cooked, breaks down and gives the beef a really soft, succulent and tender texture. Sticking the meat in a marinade for 24 hours adds bags of flavour and further improves the texture.

Short ribs with horseradish dumplings

SERVES 4

4 juniper berries
4 dried bay leaves
4 garlic cloves, grated
2 tablespoons dark muscovado sugar
2 tablespoons cracked black pepper
2 tablespoons dried sage
2 tablespoons dried rosemary
2 tablespoons dried thyme
2 tablespoons flaky sea salt
1 x 3-bone piece of short rib, about 2.5kg
400ml cider
400ml beef stock

For the dumplings
125g fresh breadcrumbs
125g self-raising flour
125g shredded suet
4 tablespoons finely chopped flat-leaf parsley
4 tablespoons freshly grated horseradish
1 egg, lightly beaten
2–3 tablespoons milk
500ml cider
500ml chicken stock
12 small turnips, peeled
50g butter
2 teaspoons cornflour
300g turnip top leaves
Salt and freshly ground black pepper

Crush the juniper berries and bay leaves together in a pestle and mortar. Place in a mixing bowl with the garlic, sugar, pepper, dried herbs and flaky sea salt. Mix together and rub into the beef on both sides. Place in a plastic container, cover and refrigerate overnight.
.....
The next day, preheat the oven to 160°C/Gas Mark 2½.
.....
Place the beef in a large, lidded casserole. Pour in the cider and beef stock. Put the lid on and stick it in the oven. Cook for 3½–4 hours, until the beef is very tender. Keep an eye on the liquid – you don't want it to boil away completely. If you need to top it up with a splash of water, go ahead.
.....
When the beef is tender, remove the lid, return the beef to the oven and cook for a further 30–40 minutes until the beef starts to take on some colour, like a roast. Baste it with the remaining liquid from the bottom of the casserole to give it a nice glaze. Remove from the oven and rest on a warm plate for 30 minutes before serving, covered lightly with foil to help retain the heat.
.....
Meanwhile, make the dumplings by combining the breadcrumbs, flour, suet, parsley, horseradish and a pinch of salt in a mixing bowl. Make a well in the centre. Whisk the egg and milk together and add them to the dry ingredients. Mix until you have a soft dough. Shape into 8 dumplings.
.....
Continues overleaf

Short ribs with horseradish dumplings

Continued

Preheat the oven to 180°C/Gas Mark 4. Pour the cider and chicken stock into a casserole and bring to the boil. Turn the heat down to a simmer and gently lower the dumplings into the stock. Pop the lid on and stick it in the oven for 15 minutes, until the dumplings have doubled in size. Remove the casserole from the oven (but leave the oven on) and carefully lift the dumplings out with a slotted spoon. Drain on kitchen paper.

·····

Put the casserole on a high heat and bring to the boil. Add the turnips and cook on a high heat, until the stock has reduced by a third.

·····

Meanwhile, place the dumplings on a baking tray and roast them in the oven until they form a lovely toasted crust – this will take about 8–10 minutes.

·····

Add the butter to the boiling turnips and leave the stock to reduce a little more, letting the butter thicken and emulsify the sauce. Mix the cornflour with a splash of water, then add this to the casserole. Simmer for a few minutes and then season. Stir in the turnip tops and return the dumplings to the pan.

·····

Serve in warmed serving bowls, with the beef.

Quick, simple and packed full of dancing flavours, these sandwiches are salty, smoky and intensely savoury. The method of cooking 'black and blue' comes from the steel workers in Pittsburgh who used to take raw steaks to work. When the hot steel came out from the rollers, they would slap the meat on to it, sear it on both sides and have it for lunch. I'm using tail end fillets in this recipe as they offer good value and are so tender – just ask your butcher.

Black & blue steak sandwiches

SERVES 2

1 tablespoon flaky sea salt
2 teaspoons chilli flakes
1 teaspoon ground coriander
1 teaspoon cracked
   black pepper
1 teaspoon dried oregano
1 teaspoon ground mace
1 teaspoon dried bay leaf,
   ground to a powder
2 garlic cloves, grated
4 tablespoons vegetable oil
2 x 250g beef fillet tails,
   trimmed and cut in
   half widthways
50g butter
4 slices of ciabatta, to serve

For the salad
2 banana shallots
3 tablespoons extra
   virgin olive oil
2 tablespoons yellow
   mustard seeds, toasted
   in a dry frying pan
2 tablespoons chopped,
   salted anchovies
4 Little Gem lettuces,
   leaves separated
2 tablespoons finely
   chopped chives
Finely grated zest of 1 lemon
Splash of red wine vinegar
Salt and freshly ground
   black pepper

Stir together the flaky sea salt, chilli flakes, coriander, black pepper, oregano, mace, bay leaf and garlic. Mix into a paste with the oil.
.....
Cover a chopping board with a sheet of cling film and place the fillet tails on top. Place a second piece of cling film on top and flatten the steaks out with a rolling pin to about 1cm thick. Remove the cling film and place the steaks in the spicy, smoky marinade. Make sure that the steaks get completely covered in the oil and spice.
.....
Heat two large frying pans – one on a high heat and one on a medium heat. When hot, carefully place the steaks in the pan on the high heat and sear for 1 minute until they start to 'blacken'. Turn them over and add the butter. Cook for a further minute and remove from the pan to rest for a few minutes.
.....
Meanwhile, make the salad. Slice the shallots into thin rings. Place the olive oil in the other pan. Add the shallots, mustard seeds and anchovies. Cook for a couple of minutes until the shallots start to soften. Add the lettuce leaves and stir quickly. As they start to wilt, add the chives and lemon zest. Pour in a large splash of vinegar and season. Remove from the heat and serve with the steaks and some slices of ciabatta to soak up the juices.

Côte de boeuf is a single, large rib of beef. It's high in fat so it's very juicy and full of flavour. It's also an expensive cut, so the last thing you want to do is ruin it – the cooking method is key. Here, I cook it slowly, finishing it with a quick flash of heat to brown it. Serve the beef medium rare with a green salad and some fries. The recipe for the savoury butter makes more than you'll need but it will keep in the freezer for up to 3 months.

Côte de boeuf

SERVES 2

1 x 800g côte de boeuf,
   left at room temperature
   for 1 hour or so
Vegetable oil, for cooking
25g butter, for cooking
Salt and freshly ground
   black pepper

For the savoury brandy butter
3 juniper berries
2 cloves
1 dried bay leaf
½ teaspoon freshly
   grated nutmeg
½ teaspoon cracked
   black pepper
250g softened butter
50g Dijon mustard
25ml brandy
1 shallot, very finely diced
1 tablespoon finely
   chopped chervil
1 teaspoon finely
   chopped tarragon
½ teaspoon salt
50g bone marrow centres
   (you will need about
   200–250g bones),
   poached in water
   and chilled (optional)

To serve
Shoestring fries and
   a crisp green salad

Preheat the oven to 55°C/Gas Mark ¼, or as low as you can get your oven.

Make the savoury brandy butter. In a pestle and mortar, grind the juniper, cloves, bay leaf, nutmeg and cracked black pepper to a rough powder. Put the butter into a mixing bowl and beat with a wooden spoon or spatula. Add the ground spices, mustard, brandy, shallot, chervil, tarragon and salt and mix together. If you're using it, dice the poached bone marrow into small pieces and mix it into the butter.

Lay out a sheet of cling film on your worktop and place the brandy butter in the middle of it. Roll up into a sausage shape, about 3cm in diameter, and tie the ends of the cling film. Chill in the fridge for 1 hour or so until set. This will keep in the fridge for a week or in the freezer for up to 3 months.

Put the unseasoned rib of beef on to a flat baking tray and place in the oven. Cook for 3 hours, until the internal temperature is 55°C when tested with an instant-read thermometer. Trust me, as long as the oven is at a low enough temperature, this will be amazing!

Take the beef out of the oven and warm a large frying pan over a high heat. Pour in a little oil and the butter for cooking and heat until the butter is foaming. Season the beef heavily with salt and place it in the pan. Cook on a high heat until coloured on one side – this should take approximately 4 minutes. Flip over and colour the other side, again for about 4 minutes. While it's colouring, put a thick slice of the savoury brandy butter on to the top side and watch it melt. Take the beef from the pan and serve immediately – there's no need to rest it as the cooking process has been slow. Serve with fries and a salad, and some more of the brandy butter on the side. Lush!

Although you might think of a stew as something that is cooked over a long time, this is more of a 'stew' of flavours, which you can cook fairly quickly. I love rump steak, but you do have to use your teeth – it has great texture which means you have to chew, but you're rewarded with loads of flavour. Mushrooms are ideal companions for steak and if girolles are not in season, most types of mushroom will do.

Rump steak 'stew'

30g dried, mixed mushrooms
4 x 250g rump steak pavés
   (ask your butcher to slice
   them into pavés for you)
Vegetable oil, for cooking
50g butter
300g girolle mushrooms,
   cleaned
2 banana shallots, finely diced
2 garlic cloves, grated
400ml Beef stock (see p. 288)
50ml brandy
50ml double cream
50ml ruby port
2 plum tomatoes, blanched,
   peeled, cored, deseeded
   and diced
1 tablespoon finely
   chopped tarragon
200g broad-leaf spinach,
   tough stems removed,
   washed with some water
   still clinging to the leaves
Juice of ½ lemon
Salt and freshly ground
   black pepper

To serve
Creamy mashed potato
   or chips

Put the dried mushrooms into a bowl and pour over about 100ml of boiling water – leave them to steep and rehydrate for 20 minutes. During this time, take the rump steaks out of the fridge to come to room temperature.
.....

Warm a large, heavy-bottomed frying pan over a medium heat and drizzle in a little oil. Add 25g of the butter and heat until foaming. Season the rump steaks and fry on both sides until nicely coloured all over. Keep cooking them until they're cooked to your liking – for me, that's medium rare, which takes about 7–8 minutes in total, but fry them for longer if you want them more cooked. Remove the steaks from the pan, put them on a plate and place them in a cool oven (50°C/Gas Mark ¼, or as low as it will go) to rest until needed.
.....

Place a sieve over a bowl and drain the steeped mushrooms. Now line the sieve with muslin, place it over a clean bowl and pass the soaking liquid through it to remove any dirt. Roughly chop the mushrooms.
.....

Melt the remaining butter in the frying pan over a medium–high heat and when it foams, fry the girolles for 2–3 minutes. Add the shallots and the garlic and fry for 5 minutes or so, stirring from time to time, until softened. Add the steeped mushrooms and stir. Add 50ml of the soaking water, the beef stock and brandy and bring to the boil. Simmer to reduce the liquid by a third, then add the cream and return to the boil. Add the port then stir in the diced tomatoes and tarragon. Place the spinach on top and put a lid on the pan or cover tightly with tin foil. Turn the heat off and leave for 2 minutes.
.....

Remove the lid and stir the wilted spinach into the 'stew'. Stir in the lemon juice and season. Remove the steaks from the oven, slice into thick pieces and place in the stew, along with any resting juices. Serve on warmed plates, with creamy mashed potato or chips.

American street-food classics such as these delicious brisket sandwiches are now quite commonplace in our restaurants and bars. Done well, they're a fantastic way of cooking cheaper cuts of meat. My recipe has great, punchy flavours and the cooking process is quite easy, but the end product is different from the braised dishes and casseroles normally associated with these cuts of meat.

Pulled beef brisket in a bun

2 tablespoons coriander seeds
2 tablespoons cumin seeds
1½ tablespoons yellow
   mustard seeds
1 tablespoon black
   peppercorns
1 tablespoon dark
   muscovado sugar
1 tablespoon smoked paprika
1 teaspoon cayenne pepper
2kg whole piece of
   beef brisket
400ml Beef stock (see p. 288)

For the milk buns
600g plain flour, plus a
   little more for dusting
15g fresh yeast, crumbled
20g salt
40g caster sugar
375ml milk
30g butter
Vegetable oil, for greasing
1 egg, lightly beaten
1 teaspoon sesame seeds
1 teaspoon flaky sea salt

Preheat the oven to 190°C/Gas Mark 5. Put the coriander, the cumin and mustard seeds, and the peppercorns into an ovenproof frying pan and pop in the oven until toasted and fragrant. This should take about 5–8 minutes – be careful not to burn them! Alternatively, toast them until fragrant in a dry frying pan. Remove from the oven or pan, tip on to a plate and cool, then crush to a fine powder with a pestle and mortar. Add the sugar, paprika and cayenne pepper and mix together. Score the inside of the beef a few times with a sharp knife, then rub this mixture all over the brisket, inside and out. Roll up the joint and tie securely with string in several places. Cover with cling film and refrigerate overnight.

· · · · ·

The next day, preheat the oven to 160°C/Gas Mark 3. Pour the beef stock into a roasting tin. Rest a large, ovenproof cooling rack over the top of the tin, put the brisket on top, then cover tightly with tin foil. Cook for 4–6 hours, checking from time to time that the beef stock hasn't evaporated. If it looks a little low, add some water. The beef should be very tender. Remove from the oven and leave to rest with the tin foil on for 25 minutes.

· · · · ·

While the brisket is in the oven, make the milk buns and prepare the coleslaw. For the buns, place the flour in a stand mixer with the dough hook attachment. Add the yeast, salt and sugar. Warm the milk and butter in a small saucepan over a low heat – the butter should just melt. Add this warm mix to the flour and bring together with the dough hook. Once it comes together, continue to knead it for a further 5–8 minutes until you have a shiny, almost silky dough. Remove the bowl from the mixer and cover with cling film. Place in a warm space and leave to prove until the dough has doubled in size.

· · · · ·

For the coleslaw
4 red onions
2 Spanish onions
½ mooli (white radish)
¼ white cabbage,
   tough core removed
2 tablespoons flaky sea salt
1 bunch of spring onions,
   finely sliced
1 bunch of chives,
   finely chopped
50g mayonnaise
2 tablespoons onion seeds
2 tablespoons prepared
   English mustard
2 teaspoons cracked
   black pepper

For the barbecue sauce
250ml Cabernet Sauvignon
   vinegar
75g dark muscovado sugar
75ml bourbon
75ml cola
250ml tomato ketchup
Splash of Worcestershire
   sauce
200ml Beef gravy (see p. 289)

Once doubled in size, knock the air out of the dough with your hands and knead it. Lightly dust a surface with flour, tear off pieces of dough and roll them into balls. Place the balls on a lightly oiled baking sheet, spaced slightly apart. You should get about 12 rolls, each weighing about 80g. Leave these to prove for 40 minutes to 1 hour; the timing will depend on how warm it is in your kitchen. They will prove into each other, nudging one another lightly.

· · · · ·

Preheat the oven to 220°C/Gas Mark 7. Brush the tops of the rolls with the beaten egg. Sprinkle on the sesame seeds and the flaky sea salt. Bake for 8–12 minutes until golden. Cool on a wire rack.

· · · · ·

To make the coleslaw, slice the red onions, Spanish onions, mooli and white cabbage very thinly with a sharp knife or a Japanese mandolin and place in a large mixing bowl. Add the flaky sea salt and mix together with your hands. Leave for 20–25 minutes until the salt starts to wilt the vegetables. Place the mixture in a colander and rinse under cold running water for 2–3 minutes, then leave to drain.

· · · · ·

Pat the vegetable mixture dry with kitchen paper. Place in a clean bowl with the spring onions and chives. Mix in the mayonnaise, onion seeds, mustard and black pepper until well combined. It's now ready to serve, but it will keep, covered, for 2 days in the fridge.

· · · · ·

As the brisket begins its resting time, start to make the barbecue sauce. Pour the vinegar into a large saucepan and bring to the boil. Turn the heat down and slowly reduce the vinegar by half. Add the sugar, bourbon, cola, ketchup, Worcestershire sauce, beef gravy and any juices from the joint's roasting tray (skim off any fat first), and bring back to the boil. Turn the heat down and simmer very slowly for 15–20 minutes. Remove the brisket from the tin and, with a fork, break up all of the meat into flakes. Add the meat to the simmering pan. Bring the pan back to a very low simmer and cook for 10–15 minutes until the beef takes on the sauce and you have a luscious pan of delight. Remove from the heat.

· · · · ·

Serve the beef, barbecue sauce and coleslaw with some buns to make the ultimate sandwich. Any leftover buns can be frozen for up to 1 month.

Photographs overleaf

This is my take on that well-loved favourite, liver and bacon. The sage and onion fritters are a bit like an Indian pakora, which gives a great crispy texture to contrast with the meltingly soft and luscious calf's liver. The bacon butter is a little condiment which I'm sure you'll make again and again – you can use it in all sorts of recipes, or simply spread it on hot toast, and it freezes very well.

Calves' liver with sage & onion fritters

SERVES 2

Vegetable oil, for cooking
2 pieces of calf's liver, about 180–200g each
Some plain flour, seasoned with salt, pepper and a bit of cayenne pepper, for dusting
Juice of 1 lime
4 tablespoons sherry vinegar
4 tablespoons Meat stock base (see p. 284)
Salt and freshly ground black pepper

For the bacon butter
100g bacon trimmings, from your butcher, diced as finely as you can
250g unsalted butter
½ teaspoon smoked paprika

For the onion fritters
2 onions, halved and finely sliced
1 tablespoon flaky sea salt
1 teaspoon dried sage
3 tablespoons chopped sage
1 teaspoon Curry powder (see p. 290) or use a good-quality bought one
1 tablespoon tapioca flour
About 1 tablespoon gram flour (chickpea flour)
Vegetable oil, for deep-frying

First make the bacon butter. Warm a large saucepan over a medium–high heat and cook the bacon trimmings until the bacon starts to crisp and little bits stick to the bottom of the pan. Turn the heat down, add the butter and paprika, and stir everything together. Continue to cook until the butter starts to foam, then pass the mixture through a fine sieve into a container, discarding the bacon, and cool. When cool, seal and place in the fridge until it sets. You can freeze the bacon butter for up to 3 months.

.....

To make the fritters, place the sliced onions in a large mixing bowl and season with the flaky sea salt and dried sage. Mix together and leave to stand for 15–20 minutes, until the onions have softened. Wrap the onions in a clean tea towel and squeeze out any excess liquid over a bowl. Reserve the liquid. Put the onions back into a clean bowl and stir in the fresh sage.

.....

Stir the curry powder, tapioca flour and gram flour into the drained onion water, to form a paste which is a bit thicker than double cream – you may need to add a little more gram flour. Mix this paste with the onions to make a fritter batter.

.....

Heat the oil in a deep fat fryer to 180°C. Gently lower small spoonfuls of the fritter mixture into the oil – they should be about the size of golf balls – and cook until they are golden and crisp. Carefully remove from the fryer and drain on kitchen paper; season. You may need to cook the fritters in batches; make sure you let the oil come back up to temperature between batches. Place in a low oven to keep warm while you finish preparing the rest of the dish.

.....

Continues overleaf

Calves' liver with sage
& onion fritters
Continued

For the spinach
Knob of butter
80g broad-leaf spinach,
   tough stalks removed,
   rinsed with some water
   still clinging to the leaves
Few gratings of nutmeg

To finish
2 rashers of streaky bacon

Warm a large, non-stick frying pan over a medium heat and drizzle
in a little oil. Dust the pieces of calf's liver with seasoned flour and
shake off any excess. Place them in the pan. When coloured on one
side, which will take 2–3 minutes, flip over and add 2 tablespoons of
the bacon butter to the pan. Baste the liver. Squeeze in the lime juice
and baste again. When cooked – about 4 minutes in total – put the
liver on a warm plate to rest for a couple of minutes. Place the pan
back on the heat, and add the sherry vinegar and meat stock base
to the butter left in the pan. Season and whisk together. Keep warm.
.....

To make the spinach, melt the butter in a saucepan over a medium
heat, add the spinach, put the lid on and cook for a couple of minutes
until wilted. Grate on some nutmeg, season with salt and drain.
.....

Cook the bacon rashers over a medium–high heat in a non-stick
frying pan until crisp.
.....

Place some wilted spinach on a warmed plate and then put a piece
of calf's liver on top. Dress the liver with the bacon butter sauce and
then garnish with the sage and onion fritters and crisp bacon rashers.
Repeat with the second piece of calf's liver and serve immediately.

Even though this North African-flavoured dish is a slow roast, it works well in the summer, perfect for sharing with friends over lunch in the garden. There's very little to do at the last minute so you can enjoy yourself. Harissa paste is readily available to buy, but it's fun to make your own so give it a go. You can use it to flavour all sorts of things, from fish to chickpeas and aubergines.

Slow-roast harissa lamb with lime couscous

SERVES 4–6

1 whole leg of lamb on
the bone, about 2kg
10 red onions, peeled
and halved
300ml chicken stock
4 tablespoons chopped
coriander

For the harissa
20 dried red chillies
70ml olive oil, plus a little
more for sealing the jar
6 garlic cloves, grated
2 tablespoons red
wine vinegar
2 teaspoons ground
coriander
2 teaspoons ground cumin
2 teaspoons ground
caraway seeds
2 teaspoons smoked paprika
1 teaspoon salt

First make the harissa. Place the dried chillies in a bowl and pour over just enough boiling water to cover. Cover the bowl with cling film and leave to cool. When cold, remove any stalks from the chillies and pat them dry on kitchen paper. Keep the soaking water.
.....

Place the chillies in a food processor with the rest of the harissa ingredients and blitz to a purée. If it's a bit thick, stir in a little of the soaking water. Scrape into a cold, sterilised jar (see p. 39 for how to sterilise a jar), drizzle on a little olive oil to cover the surface and seal. It will keep for up to a month in the fridge.
.....

Make cuts all over the lamb, about 10–15 cuts in all, each one about 1cm deep and 3–5cm long. Rub 3–4 tablespoons of harissa paste all over the joint, making sure you massage it right into the meat.
.....

Place all of the red onions in a large roasting tin and put the leg of lamb on top. Wrap the whole tin in cling film and place in the fridge to marinate for at least 8 hours, or overnight.
.....

Preheat the oven to 140°C/Gas Mark 1. Unwrap the cling film from the tin and place the tin in the oven. Roast for 4–5 hours, basting from time to time, until you can prise the lamb away from the bone with a fork. Lift the lamb out and place on a board or serving plate.
.....

Continues overleaf

Slow-roast harissa lamb with lime couscous

Continued

For the couscous
100ml extra virgin olive oil
Pinch of saffron threads
1 onion, finely diced
2 garlic cloves, grated
400ml water
2 chicken stock cubes
6 kaffir lime leaves
400g couscous
4 tablespoons roughly
   chopped flat-leaf
   parsley leaves
4 tablespoons roughly
   chopped coriander leaves
2 tablespoons roughly
   chopped mint leaves
100g black olives,
   pitted and halved
Finely grated zest
   and juice of 1 lemon
Salt and freshly ground
   black pepper

Pour the chicken stock into the roasting tin with the charred and soft onions. Place on the hob and bring to the boil. Scrape the bottom of the tin with a wooden spoon, if you need to, to release the flavoursome brown bits at the bottom. Bubble to reduce the stock by a third until you have a thick, rich onion sauce. Stir in 1 tablespoon of harissa and the coriander.

.....

To make the couscous, pour 50ml of the olive oil into a saucepan. Add the saffron and let it steep in the oil over a low heat for 5 minutes. Raise the heat slightly, add the onion and garlic and sweat gently until soft, stirring from time to time – about 10–15 minutes.

.....

In a separate saucepan, bring the 400ml of water to the boil. Crumble in the chicken stock cubes and the lime leaves. And while we're here, don't feel bad about using the stock cubes – good ones are ace for home cooking!

.....

Add the couscous to the onion and saffron mix and stir. Pour on the chicken stock and lime leaf mixture. Remove the pan from the heat and cover with cling film. Leave to absorb the stock for 10 minutes. Gently fluff everything up with a fork.

.....

Stir in the parsley, coriander and mint, then the olives and 2–3 tablespoons of harissa paste. Finally add the remaining olive oil, lemon zest and juice and season if needed. Serve with the lamb and the roasted onion gravy.

These look so impressive and yet they're really very easy. When you've mastered the filo folding technique, I bet you'll want to experiment with different fillings and seasonings too. They make a great light lunch with the simple cucumber salad or brilliant canapés and party food.

Moroccan lamb parcels

MAKES 12-14 PARCELS

100g couscous
1 chicken stock cube
500g minced lamb
Vegetable oil, for cooking
2 onions, finely diced
6 garlic cloves, grated
2 teaspoons ground turmeric
1 teaspoon cumin seeds
200ml chicken stock
80g sultanas
4 tablespoons finely
    chopped coriander
100g feta cheese, diced
1 x 250g packet of filo pastry
150g butter, melted
1 tablespoon icing sugar
½ teaspoon ground cinnamon
Salt and freshly ground
    black pepper

For the salad
2 cucumbers, halved
    lengthways, deseeded
    and diced
1 small bunch of mint leaves,
    roughly torn
1 small bunch of coriander,
    leaves picked; stalks
    finely chopped
Splash of red wine vinegar
4 tablespoons extra virgin
    olive oil

To serve
Plain yoghurt

Tip the couscous into a bowl and boil the kettle. Crumble the chicken stock cube over the couscous and pour on enough boiling water just to cover. Mix with a fork, cover with cling film and leave to stand for 5–10 minutes.

.....

Preheat the oven to 190°C /Gas Mark 5. Spread the minced lamb out on a baking tray and roast in the oven, stirring a couple of times to break it up, until it's well browned and crisp. This should take 15–20 minutes. Drain in a colander and discard the lamb fat.

.....

Warm a heavy-bottomed saucepan over a medium heat and pour in a splash of oil. Add the onions and garlic and sweat gently for 10–15 minutes, stirring from time to time, until soft. Stir in the turmeric and cumin and cook for a further 3–4 minutes. Add the drained mince and cover with the chicken stock. Bring to the boil and reduce until there is almost no liquid remaining in the pan. At this point, stir in the sultanas and couscous, remove from the heat and cool. When cold, stir in the coriander and feta cheese. Season to taste.

.....

Preheat the oven to 190°C /Gas Mark 5. Make the parcels. Cut the sheets of filo in half lengthways. Lay out a sheet of filo and brush it with the melted butter. Place a second one on top. Place a spoonful of the filling in one corner of the pastry, leaving a border of about 1cm around it. Carefully lift the corner of the pastry and fold on the diagonal to create a neat triangle. Continue folding the triangle, so the filling is encased in several layers of filo. As you finish each parcel, brush with a little more butter and place on a baking tray lined with baking parchment. Repeat the process until all the mixture is used up. Dust the filo parcels with the icing sugar and ground cinnamon. Bake for about 25 minutes, until golden brown and crisp.

.....

While the parcels are baking, mix together the cucumber, mint and coriander and, just before serving, dress with the vinegar and olive oil and season to taste with salt and black pepper. Serve the parcels with the salad and some yoghurt trickled over the top.

This is a great dish to cook slowly over the coals on a low barbecue, but it still works well cooked in the oven – it just won't have the smoky taste. The capers and cornichons are a perfect foil for the richness of the lamb breast.

Breast of lamb with caper & mustard glaze

SERVES 2-4

2 tablespoons flaky sea salt
1 tablespoon cracked
   black pepper
1 whole breast of lamb,
   bone in, about 1.2–1.5kg
75g capers in brine, drained
75g cornichons
6 tablespoons Dijon mustard
6 garlic cloves, 3 grated
   and 3 sliced
Finely grated zest and juice
   of 1 lemon
6–8 small red onions,
   peeled and halved
2 large green peppers,
   cored, deseeded and
   roughly chopped –
   you want to keep them
   quite chunky
1 head of fennel,
   roughly chopped
½ loaf sourdough bread,
   broken into 2cm pieces
2 tablespoons chopped
   flat-leaf parsley
2 tablespoons finely
   chopped mint
2 tablespoons finely
   chopped oregano
Splash of red wine vinegar
   (optional)

Mix the flaky sea salt and the cracked black pepper together, then rub this into the lamb breast. Place in a container or on a plate, then place in the fridge for 3–4 hours to cure. Remove from the fridge and rub off the excess salt mixture, but don't wash the lamb.
.....
Preheat the oven to 140°C/Gas Mark 1. Put a grill rack into a roasting tin and put the lamb breast on top. Roast in the oven for 3 hours.
.....
While the lamb is cooking, tip the capers and cornichons on to a chopping board and, with a sharp knife, chop them together until they are almost a purée. Put them into a mixing bowl with the mustard, grated garlic, and lemon zest and juice to make a glaze.
.....
Remove the lamb from the oven. Spread the caper glaze over the top and then return to the oven for a further hour.
.....
Take the lamb out of the oven. Gently lift the rack from the tin and drain about 90ml of the rendered lamb fat (the fat that has run out of the meat) into a bowl. Keep this to one side. Add the red onions, peppers, fennel and sliced garlic to the remaining fat and juices in the tin and mix together. You can use other vegetables if you prefer – potatoes, courgettes and aubergines work just as well. Return the lamb and veg to the oven for a further 30 minutes. Remove the tin from the oven and lift the lamb off.
.....
Mix the sourdough bread and the reserved lamb fat in a bowl and put the 'croutons' on top of the vegetables – rest them on top, don't mix them together as the bread will go soggy. Turn the oven up to 200°C/Gas Mark 6 and put the tin back in until the sourdough goes crisp. This will take 10–15 minutes. Remove the tin from the oven and stir in the herbs, saving a handful to sprinkle on top of the lamb breast.
.....
Serve straight away, using the roasting juices as a sauce. You may want to give these a splash of red wine vinegar to cut through the richness.

This dish has a proper taste of Wales; it contains two of its finest exports – lamb and laverbread. I find it astonishing that lamb necks are so often overlooked. They have the perfect fat-to-meat ratio and, cooked slowly, are succulent and tender. Many Welsh companies now sell laverbread online so there's no reason you should be deprived of its softly savoury seaweed flavour, no matter where you live.

Braised neck of lamb with toasted barley

SERVES 2

Vegetable oil, for cooking
2 whole necks of lamb, about 800g, on the bone, windpipe removed (you can ask your butcher to do this for you)
2 tablespoons Dijon mustard
2 tablespoons finely chopped fresh rosemary leaves
1 tablespoon chopped salted anchovies
Finely grated zest of 1 lemon
1 large bunch of thyme
8 red onions, halved and finely sliced
2 tablespoons redcurrant jelly
300ml chicken stock
75ml red wine vinegar

Warm a non-stick frying pan over a medium heat, add a little oil and sear the lamb necks, making sure that they get an even, dark colour all over. Remove from the pan and leave to cool at room temperature.

.....

In a small bowl, mix together the mustard, rosemary, anchovies and lemon zest. Rub this mixture all over the lamb necks. Divide the bunch of thyme in two, place a piece of lamb neck in the middle of each bundle and surround with the thyme. Secure the thyme with kitchen string, wrapping it around the pieces of neck several times.

.....

Preheat the oven to 120°C/Gas Mark ½.

.....

Warm a large casserole over a medium heat and drizzle in a little oil. Add the red onions and sweat gently until softened a bit. Stir in the redcurrant jelly, then the chicken stock and the red wine vinegar and bring to the boil. Add the lamb necks and put the lid on. Place in the oven. I know this temperature is low, but trust me, with lamb necks, the lower and longer, the better. Cook the lamb for 6 hours. After this time, check if it flakes away from the bone easily or if it needs more stock. You may need to cook it longer, until it's really tender and falling from the bone.

.....

When it's ready, remove from the oven and if you want to thicken the cooking gravy, remove the lamb from the casserole, place the casserole on a medium–high heat and simmer until the liquid has reduced and thickened. Return the lamb to the casserole, put the lid on and leave the lamb in the liquid to keep warm.

.....

For the pearl barley
150g pearl barley
50g butter
1 onion, finely diced
300ml real ale – something
    you would be happy to
    drink alongside it
250ml chicken or lamb stock
100g goat's cheese, diced
4 tablespoons crumbled
    laverbread (or nori
    seaweed sheets)
1 tablespoon thyme leaves
Salt and freshly ground
    black pepper

To serve
Sprouting broccoli or
    savoy cabbage, simply
    dressed in butter,
    salt and black pepper

Increase the oven setting to 210°C /Gas Mark 7. Scatter the pearl barley on a baking tray and bake in the oven until it smells fragrant and looks toasted and brown. This will take around 5–8 minutes. Remove the barley from the oven.

.....

Melt the butter in a large saucepan over a medium heat and sweat the diced onion gently for 10–15 minutes until soft, stirring from time to time. Add the toasted barley and pour on the ale. Bring to the boil then turn the heat down to a simmer. As the ale gets absorbed by the barley, add the chicken stock and slowly cook the barley as if it were a risotto, stirring frequently. This will take 45–50 minutes.

.....

When cooked, remove from the heat and stir in the cheese, laverbread and thyme; season.

.....

Remove the string and thyme from the lamb necks and flake the meat from the bone. You could even stir the red onions into the pearl barley if you like.

.....

Serve the lamb and pearl barley with the red onion cooking gravy from the casserole and some sprouting broccoli or savoy cabbage.

Photograph overleaf

Surely shepherd's pie deserves to be one of the great British classic dishes, but it's often the butt of people's jokes because of crimes committed in the name of school dinners and staff canteen lunches. Forget all the horror stories – done properly, with a little care and some great ingredients, it's fantastic comfort food we can justifiably be proud of.

Shepherd's pie

SERVES 4–6

2 lamb shanks
100g plain flour, for dusting
Vegetable oil, for frying
4 celery sticks, tough strings removed, finely diced
4 carrots, finely diced
2 onions, finely diced
4 garlic cloves, grated
4 teaspoons ground mace
3 fresh bay leaves
600ml Rich chicken stock (see p. 285)
500g minced lamb
4–5 rosemary sprigs, tied together with kitchen string
100ml red wine vinegar
2 tablespoons prepared English mustard
Salt and freshly ground black pepper

Dust the lamb shanks with the flour and shake off the excess. Warm a large, non-stick frying pan over a medium–high heat, add a splash of oil and fry the shanks until they're browned and caramelised all over. Remove from the pan and keep to one side.
......
Preheat the oven to 150°C/Gas Mark 2.
......
Warm a casserole over a medium heat, pour in a little oil and add half the celery, carrots, onion and garlic. Cook gently, stirring from time to time, until they start to soften – about 5–6 minutes. Add the mace and the bay leaves. Place the lamb shanks on top of the vegetables, pour on the chicken stock and bring to the boil. Place a lid on and braise in the oven for 3½ hours, until the lamb comes away from the bone very easily. Remove from the oven and leave to rest for 1 hour.
......
Turn the oven up to 200°C/Gas Mark 6. Spread the minced lamb out in a roasting tin and roast in the oven until it is browned and crisp – you are looking for a fantastic dark colour all over the mince. This should take 20–25 minutes and you should stir it a couple of times while cooking. Drain the meat in a colander and discard the fat.
......
Lift the lamb shanks from the stock and, with a fork, flake the meat from the bone and reserve. Strain the lamb braising liquor through a fine sieve and reserve. Wash out the casserole then warm over a medium–high heat. Pour in a little cooking oil, add the remaining diced vegetables and garlic, and sweat gently until they start to soften – about 4–5 minutes. Add the minced lamb, flaked lamb shanks and rosemary. Pour on the red wine vinegar and simmer until it has almost completely evaporated.
......

For the mashed potato
1.5kg floury potatoes
   (such as King Edward
   or Maris Piper), peeled
   and cut into even chunks
   of about 4cm
100ml milk
100g butter
75g grated Parmesan cheese
   or 75g diced goat's cheese
Paprika, to dust
Freshly ground white pepper

To serve
Buttered green vegetables

Pour in the lamb shank braising liquor, bring to the boil, then turn the heat down to a low simmer and cook very slowly, stirring now and again, until you have a thick, rich meat sauce. This will take around 2 hours – keep an eye on it and make sure it doesn't get too dry. Remove from the heat and stir in the mustard. Season, spoon into an ovenproof serving dish and leave to cool. Place the dish in the fridge to chill for a couple of hours or overnight.

· · · · ·

Preheat the oven to 180°C/Gas Mark 4.

· · · · ·

Bring a large saucepan of salted water to the boil. Add the potatoes to the water, turn the heat down to a low simmer and cook them for about 14–15 minutes, until soft. Drain the potatoes in a colander and leave them to steam and dry for 5 minutes. Heat up the milk and butter together in a saucepan, until the butter melts. Put the potatoes back into the saucepan they were cooked in and mash them with a potato masher, or pass them directly into the pan through a potato ricer. Gradually add the warm milk and butter and mix with a wooden spoon until it's all incorporated. Season with salt and white pepper. Place the mash on top of the chilled lamb mixture – you can spread it all over or pipe it on, whatever you like. Scatter the Parmesan or goat's cheese on top and sprinkle on a dusting of paprika.

· · · · ·

Bake for 30–35 minutes, until the cheese is bubbling and browned and the middle is hot. Serve with some buttered green vegetables.

For me, this is the ultimate slow-cooked curry: perfect for Saturday nights in or lazy, late Sunday lunches with some mates and a few cold beers. Any leftover lamb is great piled into pitta bread for a quick and tasty lunch.

Slow-cooked leg of lamb with sag aloo

SERVES 4-6

60g Curry powder (see p. 290)
2 tablespoons chilli flakes
1 tablespoon salt
90ml distilled white vinegar
1 whole leg of lamb on the
   bone, about 2kg
4 onions, halved
   and thinly sliced
500ml water

For the sag aloo
Vegetable oil, for frying
1 teaspoon cumin seeds
1 onion, halved
   and thinly sliced
3 large waxy potatoes (such as
   Charlotte), about 200g each,
   peeled and cut into 2cm dice
4cm piece of fresh ginger,
   peeled and grated
1 garlic clove, grated
1 teaspoon ground turmeric
1 teaspoon Curry powder
   (see p. 290)
500g broad-leaf spinach, tough
   stems removed, washed
   and with some water still
   clinging to the leaves
Salt

For the seasoned yoghurt
250g plain yoghurt
5–6 mint sprigs, tough
   stalks removed, chopped
Juice of ½ lemon
1½ teaspoons icing sugar
1 teaspoon ground turmeric

In a small bowl, mix together the curry powder, chilli flakes and salt then stir in the distilled vinegar to make a paste. Rub all over the lamb, place in a dish, cover with cling film and put in the fridge to marinate for at least 2 hours but preferably overnight.

.....

Preheat the oven to 150°C/Gas Mark 2.

.....

Layer the bottom of a large roasting tin with the sliced onions and place the leg of lamb on top. Pour in the water, cover with tin foil, place in the oven and cook for 4 hours. Remove the tin foil and continue to cook for a further 30–40 minutes, until the onions are soft and dark in colour and most of the liquid has evaporated. Remove from the oven and leave to rest for 20–25 minutes.

.....

While the lamb is resting, make the sag aloo. Warm a large, non-stick frying pan over a medium heat. Pour in a splash of oil, stir in the cumin seeds and fry just until they start to pop. Add the onion and cook until it starts to take on some colour – about 10–15 minutes. Add the potatoes, ginger, garlic, turmeric and curry powder. Gently stir and cook until the potato starts to soften. Pour in 300ml water and cook, stirring from time to time, until the potatoes are soft and most of the liquid has evaporated – this will take about 15 minutes. Stir in the spinach and cook until it's wilted. Season with salt and put in a warm serving bowl.

.....

Mix together all of the ingredients for the seasoned yoghurt. Flake the lamb from the bone and serve with its slow-roasted onions, the sag aloo and the seasoned yoghurt spooned over the top.

These lovely lamb cutlets make perfect finger food, but they also work really well as a posh main course. Serve them with new potatoes and a great, garlicky mayonnaise for an elegant spring lunch, or with ratatouille for something with more of the flavours of high summer – it really is a very versatile little dish.

Breaded lamb cutlets with caper butter

SERVES 2

150g plain flour
1 teaspoon paprika
1 teaspoon cayenne pepper,
    plus more to season
2 eggs, lightly beaten
150g panko breadcrumbs
6 lamb chops, French
    trimmed (you can ask your
    butcher to do this for you)
Vegetable oil, for cooking
75g butter
2 banana shallots,
    finely diced
1 tablespoon small capers
    in brine, drained
1 tablespoon cornichons,
    finely chopped
Juice of ½ lemon
2 tablespoons finely
    chopped flat-leaf parsley
Salt and freshly ground
    black pepper

To serve
Garlic mayonnaise
    and new potatoes

Mix together the flour, paprika and cayenne pepper, and tip the mixture on to a plate. Next, put the beaten eggs on a second plate, and the panko breadcrumbs on a third. Line them up side by side. One by one, dip the lamb chops into the seasoned flour, then the beaten egg and finally into the breadcrumbs. Place them on a tray, ready to cook.

.....

Warm a large, non-stick frying pan over a medium heat and pour in a thin layer of oil. Place the lamb chops in the pan and fry until golden brown on one side; this will take about 3–4 minutes. Turn over and repeat the process on the other side. Don't cook the chops on too high a heat or the breadcrumbs will brown before the lamb has a chance to cook; similarly, if you cook them too slowly, they won't crisp up and will just go soggy.

.....

When cooked, remove the chops from the pan and drain them on kitchen paper. Season to taste with salt and cayenne pepper.

.....

Pour away any leftover oil from the pan and wipe it out with kitchen paper. Put it back on a medium heat and add the butter. Increase the heat to high and just as the butter starts to brown, add the shallots, capers and cornichons. Stir around and add the lemon juice. Season and throw in the parsley.

.....

Divide the lamb chops between two serving plates and spoon the sauce over the top. Add a dollop of garlic mayonnaise to each plate and serve with some new potatoes alongside.

If you're stuck for a weeknight tea, Barnsley chops are great – for a start, they're double chops so they satisfy the hungriest of appetites and their naturally sweet fat keeps them succulent and tasty. Adding the cumin and coriander, as well as the zing of orange zest at the end, makes a simple dinner a bit more special.

Barnsley chop with cumin & coriander

SERVES 2

2 tablespoons cumin seeds
2 tablespoons coriander seeds
2 thick Barnsley chops
Vegetable oil, for cooking
Generous knob of butter
Juice of ½ lemon
Finely grated zest of
    1 small orange, to garnish
Salt and freshly ground
    black pepper

To serve
Couscous, potatoes or
    rice and some simple
    steamed greens

In a dry frying pan, toast the cumin and coriander seeds until lightly toasted – about 3 minutes. Be careful not to burn them. Remove from the heat and transfer to a plate to cool. Crush the seeds in a pestle and mortar then sieve them on to a plate to get rid of any woody bits. Push one side of each Barnsley chop into the spice mixture and make sure it gets a good coating. Season with salt and pepper.

Warm a large, non-stick frying pan over a medium heat and pour in a little oil. When hot, place the lamb chops in the pan, outer-skin-and-fat-side down, so they look as if they are standing up on their sides. Hold them in place with tongs or clean fingers and cook until the fat runs out and the skin starts to brown. Pour the lamb fat into a bowl, cover and refrigerate. You can use the fat for all kinds of things, including the dressing for the Courgette and feta salad (see p. 67).

Place the chops, seasoned-side down, in the pan and cook for 8–10 minutes until dark brown and caramelised. Turn the chops over and cook for a further 2–3 minutes for medium-rare lamb. Add the butter and squeeze in the lemon juice. When the butter has melted, baste the chops then remove them from the pan and leave to rest for 5 minutes on a warm plate.

Place each chop on a warm serving plate, sprinkle over some orange zest then serve with couscous, potatoes or rice and greens alongside.

Every time I wrap a leg of lamb in loads of bay leaves, it reminds me of the sort of proper peasant cooking of the Mediterranean, unchanged for centuries. Wherever you live, put this in the oven and once the delicious smells start to waft through the house, you can almost imagine yourself in one of those simple hillside restaurants in Italy, Greece or France.

Leg of lamb with bay leaves, juniper & thyme

SERVES 4–6

2 tablespoons flaky sea salt
2 tablespoons juniper berries
1 whole leg of lamb on the
   bone, about 1.5–2kg
2 tablespoons olive oil, plus
   a little more for frying
1 bunch of thyme,
   2 tablespoons of leaves
   picked from the stems, the
   remaining stems reserved
Finely grated zest of 1 lemon
2 generous branches of fresh
   bay leaves, or lots of
   rosemary sprigs if you
   haven't got any bay leaves
1 head of celery, trimmed,
   tough strings removed,
   roughly chopped
375ml white wine
500ml Lamb, Rich chicken
   or Beef stock (see pp. 287,
   285 and 288)
25g butter

Warm the flaky sea salt and juniper in a dry frying pan over a high heat for 4–5 minutes until the salt starts to discolour and the room smells of juniper. Remove from the heat, tip on to a plate and leave to cool. Crush together using a pestle and mortar.

.....

Place the leg of lamb on a chopping board and make cuts about 1cm deep into the flesh with a sharp knife. You want to do this about 8–10 times on each side of the leg. Rub in the salt and juniper, massaging it right into the cuts. Rub over the olive oil then massage in the thyme leaves and lemon zest. Wrap the leg of lamb tightly in cling film and place in the fridge to marinate for at least 8 hours, but 24 hours would be better.

.....

When you're ready to cook the lamb, place one of the branches of bay leaves on a chopping board. Unwrap the lamb, place it on the bay leaves and then put the second branch on top. The branches should have enough leaves on them so that the lamb looks like a camouflaged tank. Tie the lamb with butcher's twine or kitchen string to secure the bay leaves.

.....

Preheat the oven to 150°C/Gas Mark 2.

.....

Stick a large roasting tin on the hob and warm over a medium heat. Pour in a little oil and add the celery. Sweat gently, stirring from time to time, until it starts to soften. Add the thyme sprigs and stir. Sit a roasting rack in the tin on top of the celery, place the leg of lamb on top and pour in the white wine and stock. Bring to the boil and cover tightly with tin foil.

.....

For the cavolo nero
100ml extra virgin olive oil
1 onion, halved
 and finely sliced
2 garlic cloves, grated
4 tablespoons chopped
 salted anchovies
2 heads of cavolo nero,
 tough stalks removed,
 roughly chopped
Finely grated zest of 1 lemon
Salt and freshly ground
 black pepper

To serve
Salt-baked garlic (see p. 239)

Put the roasting tin in the oven and braise the lamb for 4½ hours until it's tender and flakes easily from the bone. Remove from the oven and leave to rest in the tin with the foil on for 30 minutes, then gently remove the lamb from the tin and place it on a chopping board.

.....

Put the roasting tin back on the hob and boil the cooking liquor over a high heat until it is reduced by half to create lovely, fragrant lamb gravy. Add the butter towards the end of the cooking. Pass through a fine sieve, pushing as much as possible through, and keep to one side.

.....

While the lamb is resting, prepare the cavolo nero. Warm the olive oil in a large, heavy-bottomed saucepan over a medium–low heat and throw in the onion and garlic. Sweat down for about 10 minutes, until just soft, stirring from time to time. Add the anchovies and the cavolo nero and stir to wilt the leaves. Add the lemon zest and season to taste.

.....

Remove the string and the bay leaves from the joint. Blowtorch the lamb to give it a lovely, deep brown colour. Brush over a little of the gravy to glaze and serve with the salt-baked garlic, the wilted cavolo nero and the gravy in a warmed jug on the side.

Photographs overleaf

This is just a brilliant way of cooking garlic – and it's great fun to do too. If you can't find elephant garlic just use the biggest bulbs you can find, though they will have a stronger flavour. Sealing the large bulbs in the salt-dough crust makes them incredibly tender and concentrates the pungent sweetness of their flavour.

Salt-baked garlic

SERVES 4

2 large bulbs of
    elephant garlic,
    cloves separated
1 lemon
½ bunch of rosemary,
    cut into pieces
    with scissors

For the salt dough
500g plain flour, plus
    extra for dusting
150g salt
2 egg whites,
    lightly beaten
200ml water

To serve
Wilted greens
Extra virgin olive oil
Flaky sea salt

You will also need
25 x 25cm square of muslin

First make the salt dough. Put the flour in a large bowl with the salt. Add the egg white and work in the water. Knead together very heavily with your hands to form a smooth dough. You could do this in a mixer with a dough hook attachment if you prefer. Wrap the dough in cling film and place it in the fridge to rest for at least 1 hour.

Put the garlic cloves in a bowl and pour over enough boiling water to cover. Leave to cool for 15–20 minutes – this will loosen the skin. Peel all the cloves and set aside.

Preheat the oven to 200°C/Gas Mark 6 and line a baking tray with baking parchment.

On a lightly floured surface, roll out the salt dough into a circle 5mm thick. Place the piece of muslin on the dough. Score the outside of the lemon with a few deep cuts and place it in the middle of the muslin. Build up the garlic cloves around the lemon, until it looks like a giant garlic bulb. Place the rosemary all around, then wrap it up, firstly in the muslin cloth and then in the salt dough. Seal the dough at the top, pressing it together to make sure there are no gaps. Secure the top of the dough with kitchen string (see photograph on page 130).

Place on the prepared tray and put into the oven. Bake for 45 minutes.

Break open the salt crust and unravel the muslin; discard the muslin and dough. Inside, the garlic should be soft and lovely. You can roughly chop both the lemon and the garlic and stir them through some wilted greens, such as the cavolo nero served with the Leg of lamb with bay leaves (see page 234). Finish the greens simply, with just a splash of extra virgin olive oil and a sprinkling of flaky sea salt.

puddings

When I first started working in professional kitchens, one of the things that struck me as odd was how the pastry chef often worked apart from the rest of the brigade. It bothered me and it's something I've always avoided in my own kitchens.

Everyone should work together. There should be a flow, a synergy, from starter to main course to pudding. It's balanced, creative, and definitely more fun that way.

When you're putting together your own special meals, try to think of them as a whole: aim to balance the textures and flavours not just in individual dishes, but across all the courses.

In the starters chapter, I said that there's nothing wrong with serving some salami or radishes as a simple first course if you're in a rush. In the same way, when you get to the end of the meal, there's no shame in putting out some good cheese and lovely, ripe fruit. But when you do have time, it's great to seize the chance to make a grand final impression.

Almost all of the puds in this chapter can be made ahead, so there's no need to stress out about anything at the last minute. Whether you want a fruity, chocolatey or creamy end to your meal, there's something here for you. Of course, there are showstoppers, like the Grown-up doughnuts dusted with lavender sugar or the Chocolate tart, with its crunchy almond topping and boozy chocolate cream. But there are cosy, easy ideas too, such as the Risotto rice pudding, which will carry you through the seasons if you vary the fruit topping.

My final word of advice to you when it comes to puddings is to go easy on the sugar. I always strive to bring out my ingredients' natural flavours – I want them to taste as intense as possible – so it's important that sugar doesn't overpower. Too much sugar kills subtlety and your dish will simply taste sweet. Rein it in and let the flavours flourish – that's what it's all about after all...

I love the rich, warming combination of flavours here. The ginger in the biscuits and muscovado sugar in the creams go so beautifully with the lively acidity of the plums. It really is one of my favourite autumn puddings.

Sweet muscovado creams

SERVES 6

4 gelatine leaves
225ml milk
100g light muscovado sugar
1½ tablespoons black treacle
675ml double cream

For the sour plums
150g caster sugar
100ml red wine vinegar
200ml red wine
1 cinnamon stick
1 vanilla pod, split lengthways
1 lemon, zest pared into strips
    with a sharp vegetable
    peeler, any bitter white
    pith removed
400g plums, halved
    and stoned

For the gingerbread biscuits
170g self-raising flour
110g light muscovado sugar
1 tablespoon ground ginger
1 teaspoon bicarbonate
    of soda
60g butter
1 egg, lightly beaten
1 tablespoon golden syrup

Soak the gelatine in cold water for 4–5 minutes to soften. Pour the milk into a small saucepan and bring to the boil. Put the sugar and black treacle into a bowl and pour on the hot milk. Stir and cool slightly. Squeeze out the excess water from the gelatine leaves and whisk them into the warm milk mixture until the sugar and gelatine dissolve. Stir in the double cream then pass through a fine sieve into a jug. Leave to settle for 5–10 minutes then skim off any surface bubbles. Pour the mixture into six small bowls. Cover with cling film and place in the fridge to set for about 4 hours or overnight.
.....

To make the sour plums, warm the sugar and vinegar in a saucepan, stirring until the sugar dissolves, then boil until reduced by half. Add the red wine, cinnamon and vanilla. Bring to the boil, add the lemon zest and simmer for 4–5 minutes on a low heat. Put the plums into the pan, flesh-side down, and remove from the heat. Cover with a lid and leave them to cook in the residual heat for 15–20 minutes.
.....

When the plums have cooled a little, you can cut each half into two pieces ready for serving. Put them into a clean container and pour on the cooking liquid. They will keep, covered, in the fridge for up to 2 days.
.....

To make the gingerbread biscuits, place all of the dry ingredients in a large mixing bowl and add the butter, rubbing it together with your fingertips until the mixture resembles coarse crumbs. Add the egg and golden syrup and bring together to form a stiff paste. Wrap in cling film and chill in the fridge for at least 1 hour or up to a day.
.....

Continues overleaf

Sweet muscovado creams

Continued

When you're ready to bake the biscuits, preheat the oven to 180°C/Gas Mark 4. Line two baking sheets with baking parchment.
.....
Roll the mixture into balls between your hands; they should be about the size of walnuts and you should have enough mixture for 16–20 biscuits.
.....
Place the balls about 5cm apart on the baking sheets so they have room to spread out. Bake for 12–15 minutes, until just cooked. Remove from the oven, leave on the sheets to firm up for a couple of minutes then place on a wire rack to cool completely.
.....
To serve, place some sour plums on top of the set muscovado creams and spoon on a little of the poaching liquid. Crumble some biscuits over the top and serve with more biscuits on the side.

Hello you! In my opinion, this is probably one of the greatest puddings of our time. It's proper, cosy comfort food that's guaranteed to raise a smile. I use brioche breadcrumbs as they're a little richer than normal ones and make the tart even more indulgent. I'm really fond of the pastry here: using bran flakes gives it an interesting flavour and it works very well as an alternative in many sweet tart recipes.

Treacle tart with mascarpone ice cream

MAKES A 24CM TART

225g butter
675g golden syrup
190g fresh brioche crumbs
  (see p. 128 for how
  to prepare these)
75ml double cream
2 eggs and 1 egg yolk,
  lightly beaten
½ teaspoon salt
Good pinch of flaky
  sea salt, to finish

For the pastry
250g softened butter
100g caster sugar
250g plain flour, sifted,
  plus a little more
  for dusting
190g bran flakes,
  blended to a powder
  in a food processor
Pinch of salt
2 eggs, lightly beaten

For the mascarpone ice cream
250g mascarpone cheese
225g double cream
150ml milk
100g caster sugar
½ vanilla pod, split
  lengthways, seeds
  scraped out
Pinch of salt

To make the ice cream, mix all of the ingredients together in a bowl until well combined and very smooth, then churn in an ice-cream machine according to the manufacturer's instructions. Place the mixture in a freezer container and freeze until needed. Remove from the freezer about 10 minutes before you want to serve it.

.....

Next make the pastry. Cream together the butter and sugar. Fold in the flour, powdered bran flakes and salt. Add the eggs and mix to form a paste. Wrap in cling film and place in the fridge to rest for at least 1 hour, or up to a day.

.....

Preheat the oven to 170°C/Gas Mark 3.

.....

On a lightly floured surface, roll out the pastry to the thickness of a £1 coin. Use the pastry to line a 24cm loose-bottomed tart tin, gently pressing the pastry all of the way in and letting the excess hang over the sides. Line the inside with baking parchment or several layers of cling film and pour in some ceramic baking beans, uncooked rice or dried pulses to fill the base. Place the tin on a baking sheet and bake for 20–25 minutes. Remove from the oven, take out the parchment and beans and return to the oven to cook for a further 10 minutes until the tart shell is cooked through and dried out. Leave to cool.

.....

Continues overleaf

Treacle tart with mascarpone ice cream

Continued

Lower the oven temperature to 160°C/Gas Mark 2½. To make the filling, melt the butter in a saucepan over a medium heat until it foams and turns a nutty, golden brown. Whisk in the golden syrup, which will stop the butter from cooking further. Take the pan off the heat, pass the mixture through a fine sieve to remove any solids and set aside.

.....

Mix the brioche crumbs in a medium-sized bowl with the butter and syrup mixture. Whisk in the cream, whole eggs, egg yolk and salt, and leave to cool for 10–15 minutes. Pour into the tart case and place on a baking sheet in the oven to cook for 25 minutes.

.....

Reduce the oven setting to 140°C/Gas Mark 1 and cook for a further 30 minutes, until the tart is just set – it should still have a little wobble to it in the centre.

.....

Remove from the oven and leave to cool. When ready to serve, sprinkle a little flaky sea salt over the top of the tart, trim the top edges, release the ring and place on a serving plate. Serve with the mascarpone ice cream.

This is an easy but very tasty dessert. For a change, I use risotto rice rather than pudding rice so it cooks quicker but I toast it first for a richer, malty taste. Adding some chopped peaches and a dollop of cinnamon crème fraîche at the end makes this pudding even more special – I predict its simplicity and flavour will make it one of your go-to desserts.

Risotto rice pudding

SERVES 6

125g Arborio rice
50g skinned almonds, chopped
50g butter
450ml double cream
350g almond milk, unsweetened
75g dark muscovado sugar
2 tablespoons mascarpone cheese

For the crème fraîche
150g crème fraîche
1 tablespoon icing sugar
1 teaspoon ground cinnamon
Finely grated zest of ½ orange

To finish
3 ripe peaches, diced
3 mint sprigs, leaves picked, roughly torn
2 tablespoons light muscovado sugar

Preheat the oven to 200°C/Gas Mark 6. Put the rice on a baking tray and bake for about 15 minutes, until it turns golden brown and smells toasted. Put the almonds on a second tray and toast them too; this should take about 4–5 minutes – keep an eye on them, as they burn quickly. When the rice and almonds are toasted, remove them from the oven and leave to cool.
.....
Melt the butter in a large, heavy-bottomed saucepan over a medium-high heat and cook until it starts to foam and turn a rich, nutty brown. Add the rice, turn the heat down and stir until the rice is covered in the browned butter. Pour in the cream, almond milk and dark muscovado sugar. Gently cook the rice for about 15–20 minutes, stirring all the time, until it softens and absorbs the creamy liquid. Stirring helps release the starches from the rice, which thickens the cream. Remove from the heat, stir in the toasted almonds and leave to rest for 4–5 minutes. Stir in the mascarpone.
.....
While the pudding is resting, whisk together the crème fraîche, icing sugar, cinnamon and orange zest until it's nice and thick.
.....
Either spoon the pudding into a large serving dish or into individual bowls. Scatter some peaches and mint over the top, then spoon over several dollops of the crème fraîche if serving from a large dish, or place one dollop in each bowl. Sprinkle on a little light muscovado sugar and serve.

I know this might sound a little bizarre, but think of this as a raspberry cheesecake with no biscuit base... There, it's not too bad now is it?

Raspberry rose water jellies with sweet cheese

SERVES 6

400g raspberries
450ml sparkling
 white wine
Juice of 1 lemon
100g caster sugar
8 gelatine leaves
1–2 tablespoons rose
 water, to taste

For the honeycomb
170g caster sugar
65g glucose syrup
25g runny honey
2 tablespoons water
1 teaspoon bicarbonate
 of soda

For the sweet cheese
100g mascarpone cheese
100g cream cheese
50g caster sugar
1 tablespoon thyme leaves

Put 200g of the raspberries into a blender or food processor with the sparkling wine and purée until smooth. Add the lemon juice and the sugar and blend again. Pass this mixture through a fine sieve into a jug. Soak the gelatine leaves in a bowl of cold water until they go soft – about 4–5 minutes.
.....
Add the rose water to the raspberry liquid to taste. Go carefully, as it's strong – start with a little and build up to the flavour you like.
.....
Wring out the excess water from the gelatine, place it in a small saucepan and heat very gently, stirring a couple of times, until it has melted. This shouldn't take more than 30 seconds. Remove from the heat immediately, pour the melted gelatine into the raspberry liquid and mix thoroughly.
.....
Divide the remaining raspberries between six glasses or serving bowls. Pour the jelly mixture over the top, cover and put them in the fridge to set. This should take about 4 hours. You can make the jellies the day before you want to serve them if you like.
.....
While the jellies are setting, make the honeycomb. Line a baking tray with baking parchment. Put the sugar, glucose syrup, honey and water into a large saucepan and heat, stirring to dissolve the sugar, until it reaches 150°C on an instant-read thermometer. Whisk in the bicarbonate of soda – watch out, the mixture will foam and puff up. Immediately, pour the mixture on to the lined baking tray and leave it to cool.
.....
To make the sweet cheese, beat all of the ingredients together until soft and smooth.
.....
To serve, spoon some sweet cheese over each of the jellies then sprinkle some crushed honeycomb on top.

I've given that classic combination of airy meringue and tropical fruits an extra kick with a swirl of rum and vanilla cream. Make these pavlovas in individual portions as I've done here, or one large one – put it in the middle of the table and let everyone dive in and help themselves.

4 kiwi fruits
2 mangoes
1 papaya
1 banana
¼ pineapple
4 passion fruit
Juice and finely grated
    zest of 2 limes
4–6 mint sprigs, leaves
    only, finely shredded

For the meringues
4 egg whites
225g caster sugar
1 tablespoon white
    wine vinegar
2 teaspoons cornflour

For the rum cream
350ml double cream
75g caster sugar
70ml dark rum
2 vanilla pods, split
    lengthways, seeds
    scraped out
Finely grated zest of 1 lime

Tropical fruit pavlovas

Preheat the oven to 120°C/Gas Mark ½. Line a baking sheet with baking parchment or a silicon baking mat.
.....
First make the meringues in a stand mixer or using a hand-held electric whisk. Put the egg whites in a scrupulously clean bowl and whisk them until they reach soft peaks. Add the caster sugar a spoonful at a time, whisking well after each addition, until the mixture is glossy and thick. Add the vinegar and cornflour and whisk again briefly to incorporate.
.....
With a large metal spoon, place 6 roughly shaped individual meringues on the lined baking sheet, allowing space between each one for them to expand, as they're going to be quite large. Bake for 1½ hours until they are crisp then turn the oven off, open the door and leave the meringues in the oven to dry out. When they are cold, remove them from the tray and place them on a wire rack.
.....
In a large bowl, whisk the cream, sugar, dark rum, vanilla seeds and lime zest until the mixture is thick and firm, though be careful not to overbeat.
.....
Cut the kiwi fruit, mangoes, papaya, banana and pineapple into 5mm dice and mix together in a large bowl. Cut the passion fruit in half and scrape the seeds into the bowl with a teaspoon. Add the lime juice and zest and stir. Sprinkle over the mint and mix it all together.
.....
Spoon some of the rum cream on top of a meringue and add the diced fruits. Repeat with the rest of the meringues and serve immediately.

These look like classic strawberry tarts, but of course I've tuned them up a bit – the crème patissière has cracked black pepper and some rich, sweet balsamic vinegar through it, and the garnish is basil, not mint. Trust me, they are amazing! When you're shopping for the balsamic, hunt out the best quality you can find – it'll make all the difference to the end result. I like to use fantastic eight-year-old stuff; it's lush!

Strawberry tartlets with easy strawberry ice cream

MAKES 6 TARTLETS

For the strawberry ice cream
1kg strawberries, hulled
    and halved
500ml single cream
200g caster sugar

For the sweet pastry
250g softened butter
120g caster sugar
400g plain flour, plus
    more for dusting
1 egg, lightly beaten

For the crème patissière
580ml milk
6 egg yolks, lightly beaten
110g caster sugar
60g plain flour, sifted
90ml 8-year-old
    balsamic vinegar
1½ teaspoons cracked
    black pepper

⌄

First make the ice cream. Put the strawberries in a large pan and gently stew them over a very low heat for 15–20 minutes, stirring from time to time, until they have broken down – you don't need to add any water. Tip them into a blender or food processor and whizz until smooth. Pass them through a fine sieve and leave to cool. Weigh out 500g of the purée (if you have any left over, it's delicious used to dress a fruit salad or with yoghurt). Mix it with the single cream and sugar. Place this mix in an ice-cream machine and churn until frozen. Scrape into a freezer container, seal and freeze until needed. Remove from the freezer about 10 minutes before you want to serve it.
. . . . .
Make the pastry. Cream together the butter and sugar in a stand mixer with the beater attachment. When smooth, reduce the speed and slowly add the flour and start to bring to a paste. Just before it comes together completely, add the egg. When it has just come together into a paste, remove from the bowl and wrap in cling film. Refrigerate for at least 1 hour, or overnight.
. . . . .
Preheat the oven to 170°C/Gas Mark 3.
. . . . .
Roll out the pastry on a lightly floured surface to the thickness of a £1 coin. Cut out circles and line six 10cm loose-bottomed tart tins, pushing the pastry in tightly. Let the excess hang over the sides. Line each tart with several layers of cling film or baking parchment and fill with baking beans or uncooked rice or pulses. Place on a large baking sheet and cook for 20–25 minutes, until the pastry looks crisp and golden. Remove the beans and cling film and bake for a further 5–8 minutes to make sure the tartlet shells are dried out and have an even colour. Leave to cool.
. . . . .

For the glaze
100ml water
50g caster sugar
4 tablespoons strawberry jam
2 tablespoons 8-year-old
   balsamic vinegar
Juice of ½ lemon

To finish
400g strawberries,
   the best quality you
   can find, thinly sliced
Some baby basil or basil
   cress, to decorate

To make the crème patissière, bring the milk to the boil in a medium saucepan. In a mixing bowl or a stand mixer, whisk the egg yolks and sugar until light and fluffy, then whisk in the flour. Pour on the hot milk, whisking constantly, and then pour the mixture back into the pan. Cook over a gentle heat, stirring until it thickens, and continue to cook for a further 2–3 minutes to cook out the flour. Remove the crème patissière from the heat and pour into a stand mixer with the paddle attachment. Add the balsamic vinegar and turn on to a slow speed. Keep mixing until it cools down to a smooth paste. Add the cracked black pepper, put into a container, cover and refrigerate until needed.

. . . . .

To make the glaze, put all of the ingredients into a saucepan, bring to the boil and stir until smooth and emulsified. Pass through a fine sieve and cool.

. . . . .

To construct and finish the tarts, trim the excess pastry from the tops with a small, sharp knife and remove them from the tins. Spoon in a generous portion of the crème patissière. Place the strawberries in a ring around the top of the tarts, trying to ensure the slices overlap neatly, then brush the strawberries with the glaze. Place a lovely scoop of strawberry ice cream in the centre of each and decorate with a few baby basil sprigs. Serve immediately.

Photograph overleaf

These are one of my favourite things from my mum's recipe collection. They're a twist on your classic white meringue and the hazelnuts lend them a nice chewy texture. You can toast the hazelnuts if you like, which gives them a slightly more intense flavour, though they are very good just as they are.

Brown sugar meringues with praline cream

SERVES 6

250g demerara sugar
4 large egg whites
75g blanched hazelnuts,
    finely chopped
1 teaspoon white
    wine vinegar
Cocoa powder,
    for dusting

For the praline cream
100g blanched hazelnuts
125g caster sugar
200ml double cream
75g icing sugar, sifted
2 tablespoons brandy
30g ricotta cheese

Preheat the oven to 120°C/Gas Mark 1. Line a large baking sheet or two smaller baking sheets with baking parchment and draw twelve 8cm circles on the parchment with pencil, spaced about 4cm apart. Turn the paper over (so that you don't end up with pencil on the meringues).

.....

Blitz the demerara sugar in a food processor until it's a fine powder. Using a stand mixer or a hand mixer, whisk the egg whites in a scrupulously clean bowl until they reach the soft peak stage. Continue to whisk, adding the ground demerara sugar a spoonful at a time until it is all incorporated and the meringue is thick and glossy.

.....

With a spatula, fold in the chopped hazelnuts and the vinegar. Spoon the meringue mixture into a piping bag fitted with a 1cm round nozzle and pipe it on to the parchment, using the pencilled-in circles as your guide so that they're all a uniform shape. Bake for 1½ hours then turn the oven off and leave them to cool in the oven with the door open. When cool, remove them from the tray and place them in an airtight container until needed. You can make these up to 3–4 days ahead.

.....

Now make the praline cream. Preheat the oven to 190°C/Gas Mark 5. Put the hazelnuts on to a baking tray and cook for 8–10 minutes, until they are fragrant and lightly browned. Be careful not to burn them. Leave to cool.

.....

When cool, lay the cooked hazelnuts out on a tray lined with baking parchment. Put the sugar in a heavy-bottomed saucepan (it's best to use a pan with a light interior rather than a dark one, as it's easier to gauge the colour of the caramel) and place on a medium–high heat. Heat the sugar. Be careful not to stir it too much once it begins to melt or it may crystallise. When it becomes a clear, dark amber liquid – a caramel – immediately pour it directly on top of the toasted hazelnuts and leave it to go cold. Once cold, remove the baking parchment and blitz the praline to a fine powder in a food processor.

·····

Whip the double cream with the icing sugar and brandy in a large bowl until it forms soft peaks. In a separate bowl, beat the ricotta until soft and then gently fold the cream into the ricotta with a spatula. Fold in the powdered praline.

·····

To serve, stick two meringues together with a big dollop of the praline cream and dust with the cocoa powder. Stack them on a plate and place in the middle of the table for everyone to help themselves.

This is a fantastically warming and hearty Scottish pudding. Its name comes from the word 'cloot', which means a strip of cloth, because the pudding is wrapped in muslin before being poached. It's a great alternative to Christmas pudding and can be served hot or cold.

Clootie dumpling with ginger custard

MAKES 1 PUDDING,
ENOUGH TO SERVE 8

250g plain flour, plus
   more for dusting
2 teaspoons mixed spice
1 teaspoon ground cinnamon
1 teaspoon bicarbonate
   of soda
125g shredded suet
125g sultanas
125g currants
125g stoned, chopped dates
225g golden syrup
225ml milk
Caster sugar, for dusting

For the ginger custard
300ml milk
300ml double cream
6 cloves
7 egg yolks
75g caster sugar
2 teaspoons ground ginger

To finish
Icing sugar, for dusting

Sift the flour, mixed spice, cinnamon and bicarbonate of soda into a large bowl. Stir in the suet and dried fruit then the golden syrup. Add the milk, then get your hands in there and mix to form a soft dough.

.....

Dip a clean tea towel or large piece of muslin in boiling water then wring out. Place the tea towel or muslin (doubled over so you have two layers) on a chopping board. Dust the cloth generously with flour. Place the clootie dough in the middle of the cloth and draw the sides up to form a rough ball shape – don't wrap it too tightly as the dumpling will expand a bit as it cooks. Tie the top tightly with kitchen string.

.....

Place an inverted, heatproof plate or a trivet in the bottom of a large, deep saucepan. Place the wrapped dumpling on top and fill the pan with boiling water from the kettle until it covers the dumpling. Bring back to the boil then turn the heat down to a gentle simmer and put the lid on. Poach in the pan for 4 hours. Check a couple of times during the cooking process and top up with boiling water from the kettle if the level looks low.

.....

After 4 hours, place a large bowl of iced water by the hob. Carefully remove the pudding and quickly plunge the whole thing, still in the cloth, into the iced water. This helps release the cloth from the pudding without it sticking.

.....

Preheat the oven to 180°C/Gas Mark 4. Line a baking tray with baking parchment.

.....

Continues overleaf

Clootie dumpling
with ginger custard
Continued

Remove the cloth from the pudding, place it on the baking tray
and bake for 15 minutes to dry out and develop a light crust.
Remove from the oven, dust it with caster sugar and leave
to one side to rest.

.....

While the dumpling is resting, make the custard. Pour the milk
and cream into a saucepan with the cloves and bring to the boil.

.....

In a separate bowl, whisk the egg yolks, sugar and ginger together
until they are light and fluffy. Pour on the hot milk and cream,
whisk together then return to the pan and place it back on a gentle
heat. Cook, stirring constantly, until the mixture reads 82°C on an
instant-read thermometer or until it coats the back of a wooden
spoon. Pass the mix through a fine sieve into a warmed jug.

.....

Dust the warm clootie dumpling with icing sugar before serving
with the custard. If you don't eat it all, the custard will keep for
up to 3 days sealed in the fridge and the dumpling is also
delicious served cold.

Pineapple upside-down cake is a proper childhood memory for me, but I've given it a whole new lease of life here. Traditionally this cake is made using tinned fruit, but I like to poach a fresh pineapple in star anise, vanilla and bay leaves just to give it a bit more of a flavour kick.

Pineapple upside-down cake

SERVES 6

1 super-sweet pineapple
500ml water
200g caster sugar
2 star anise
2 bay leaves
1 vanilla pod,
  split lengthways,
  seeds scraped out
1 cinnamon stick

For the topping
150g softened butter
150g dark muscovado sugar
100g stoned, chopped dates
3 teaspoons cracked
  black pepper
50ml dark rum

For the cake
100g self-raising flour
2 teaspoons baking powder
200g softened butter,
  plus slightly more
  for buttering the tin
200g light muscovado sugar
4 eggs, lightly beaten
50ml dark rum
2 vanilla pods,
  split lengthways,
  seeds scraped out
Finely grated zest of 1 lime

Trim the outside of the pineapple and cut out all of the eyes. Shape the pineapple into a cylinder. Cut into slices; you should get about seven 2cm slices, though you will only need four to five of these. Cut the centre out of each slice with a small ring cutter and use a larger ring cutter to ensure all of the slices are a uniform shape.
.....
Pour the water into a medium saucepan and add the sugar, star anise, bay leaves, vanilla pod and seeds, and cinnamon stick. Warm and stir until the sugar dissolves then bring to the boil. Lower the pineapple rings into the liquid and turn the temperature down to a low simmer. Cook for 15–20 minutes until the pineapple is just tender. Turn the heat off and let the pineapple cool in the liquid.
.....
Lightly butter a 20cm square, solid-bottomed cake tin. Line the base and sides with baking parchment and butter the parchment. Preheat the oven to 180°C/Gas Mark 4.
.....
Make the topping. With a stand mixer, hand mixer or simply with a wooden spoon, beat together the butter and sugar until creamy. Fold in the dates and cracked black pepper.
.....
Drain the pineapple slices and place them in the cake tin. Spread the topping mixture all over the pineapple. Drizzle on the dark rum.
.....
Next, make the cake. Sift together the flour and baking powder. Using a stand mixer, hand mixer or simply with a wooden spoon, beat together the butter and sugar until creamy. Slowly beat in the sifted flour, eggs, rum and vanilla seeds (reserve the pods for making vanilla sugar or custard).
.....
Continues overleaf

Pineapple upside-down cake

Continued

For the whipped coconut cream
2 x 160ml tins coconut cream
2 tablespoons caster sugar

For the toffee sauce
75g butter
100g light muscovado sugar
30ml dark rum

Spoon the mixture into the tin and smooth it down so it's level.
Place in the oven and bake for 45 minutes. Remove from the
oven and leave to stand for 10–15 minutes, then turn it out
on to a plate, ready for serving.
.....
Whisk together the coconut cream and caster sugar until you
have a light and fluffy mixture.
.....
Make the toffee sauce. Put the butter and sugar into a medium
saucepan and warm over a medium heat. Stir until the mixture
is well combined. Stir in the rum and keep warm.
.....
Sprinkle the lime zest over the cake and serve it with the toffee
sauce and the coconut cream on the side.

Doughnuts are a favourite of mine from childhood. I remember having them at fairgrounds and at the seaside. Everything that is associated with 'good times' to me also means doughnuts!

Grown-up doughnuts

MAKES 16 DOUGHNUTS

260g strong white bread flour, plus a little extra for dusting
70ml whole milk
70ml water
20g caster sugar
20g butter, melted
20g fresh yeast, crumbled
1 large egg
1 egg yolk
Pinch of salt
Groundnut, vegetable, grapeseed or other flavourless oil, for frying

For the lavender sugar
20g dried organic lavender flowers, plus a few more for decorating
200g caster sugar

For the chocolate sauce
225g dark chocolate, about 70 per cent cocoa solids, broken into small pieces
25g butter
150ml milk
40g caster sugar
Rose water, to taste – about 1 teaspoon
150ml double cream

Put all of the dough ingredients in a stand mixer with the beater attachment and mix until combined. Continue to knead in the mixer until it's smooth and elastic – about 5–10 minutes. Transfer the dough to a clean bowl and cover with cling film. Leave to prove in the fridge overnight. The next day, remove the dough from the bowl and, on a lightly floured surface, knock it back and knead the dough for a few more minutes.
.....
Line two baking trays with floured 5cm squares of baking parchment. Divide the dough into 30g balls – they should be about the size of large walnuts. Place each ball on a separate piece of parchment, leaving space between them. Dust a little more flour over the doughnuts and leave them to prove until they almost double in size – about 40 minutes.
.....
Make the lavender sugar. Blitz the lavender in a spice grinder, small food processor or clean coffee mill until it's a fine powder then mix with the caster sugar. Pour the sugar out on to a plate.
.....
Preheat the oil in a deep fat fryer to 175°C. You may need to cook the doughnuts in batches as it's important you don't crowd the pan. Make sure the oil comes back up to temperature between each batch. Carefully lift the doughnuts off their papers on to a slotted spoon and lower them into the hot oil. Cook on each side for about 4 minutes until golden brown. Remove them from the oil with the spoon and immediately roll them in the lavender sugar, shaking off the excess. Place on kitchen paper to drain and cool.
.....
Continues overleaf

Grown-up doughnuts

Continued

Make the chocolate sauce. Put the chocolate and butter into a heatproof bowl and place over a pan of barely simmering water to melt – the bottom of the bowl should not touch the water.
.....
Pour the milk and sugar into a small saucepan and bring to the boil, stirring to dissolve the sugar. Pour on top of the melted chocolate and butter and mix together until smooth. Add the rose water and cool.
.....
In a separate bowl, lightly whip the cream until it forms soft peaks and gently fold this into the chocolate mixture with a spatula. Chill for an hour or two until it thickens to piping consistency. Fill a piping bag fitted with a small nozzle with the mixture. Push the nozzle into the side of each doughnut and fill until almost bursting with the chocolate mixture.
.....
Serve with a few more of the lavender flowers scattered over the top.

This is an ace pie. I used cherries here, but you could choose pretty much any fruit that you fancy – apples, pears and rhubarb work really well too. Just cook the fruit a little first, or even purée it. Serve this with a sorbet or ice cream made from the same fruit as you've used in the pie and you have a really stunning dessert.

Cherry & chocolate custard pie

First make the pastry according to the instructions on page 256.
·····

In a saucepan, melt the butter with the kirsch and sugar on a medium heat. Add 400g of the cherries and cook until they are very soft and broken down. This will take about 8–10 minutes. Pour the cherry mixture into a blender or food processor and whizz until smooth. Pass the purée back into the pan through a fine sieve and simmer gently to reduce the sauce until it's thickened slightly.
·····

Tip in the rest of the cherries and stir around, making sure they all get covered in the warm purée. Remove from the heat and cover the pan with cling film or a tight-fitting lid so the whole cherries can cook in their own steam. Leave the pan to cool.
·····

To make the custard, bring the milk and the vanilla pod and seeds to the boil in a saucepan. In a large bowl, whisk together the egg yolks and 120g caster sugar until light and fluffy and doubled in size. Sift the flour over the whisked egg yolks and mix together. Remove the vanilla pod from the milk, then pour the milk over the egg yolks and whisk again. Pour the mixture back into the pan and return it to a medium heat. Whisk continuously as the custard thickens to make sure you get no lumps. Take it to just below boiling point – it won't curdle like normal custard because it has flour in it, but you must cook it for 5–6 minutes to get rid of the flour taste. Take off the heat and pass the custard through a fine sieve into a bowl. Place a layer of cling film directly on top of the mixture so it doesn't form a skin and leave to cool.
·····

Continues overleaf

SERVES 6-8

50g butter
70ml kirsch
150g caster sugar
1kg cherries, stoned
70g dark chocolate,
    70 per cent cocoa
    solids, grated

For the custard
570ml milk
1 vanilla pod,
    split lengthways,
    seeds scraped out
5 egg yolks
120g caster sugar
60g plain flour

For the pastry
1 quantity of Sweet
    pastry (see p. 256)

To finish
Splash of milk
2 teaspoons caster sugar
2 teaspoons ground
    cinnamon

To serve
Ice cream or sorbet,
    ideally cherry flavour

Cherry & chocolate custard pie

Continued

On a lightly floured surface, roll out two thirds of the sweet pastry to the thickness of a £1 coin. Gently line a deep 26cm pie dish with the pastry. Try not to let the pastry crack, though if you do, you can patch it up with some pastry trimmings. Line the pie dish with baking parchment or several layers of cling film then fill with ceramic baking beans or uncooked rice or pulses. Chill in the fridge for 30 minutes.
.....
Preheat the oven to 170°C/Gas Mark 3. Bake the pie shell for 20–25 minutes, until golden – you may need to turn the tart around halfway through to ensure it's evenly cooked. Remove the baking parchment and the beans and return to the oven for a further 8–10 minutes until the pastry is a dark golden brown. Remove from the oven and cool.
.....
Turn the oven up to 190°C/Gas Mark 5. Place a sieve over a bowl and drain the cherries; reserve the liquor. Spread the cherries evenly in the pie shell. Pour in a little of the purée and mix together. Sprinkle the grated chocolate on top of the cherries.
.....
With a large spoon, distribute the custard carefully and evenly over the cherries. Smooth with a palette knife dipped in warm water.
.....
On a lightly floured surface, roll out the remaining third of the sweet pastry to the thickness of a £1 coin and place it on top of the pie. Seal around the edges. Trim the sides and pierce the top to release any steam during cooking. Brush with a little milk. Dust the top of the pie with the sugar and cinnamon and bake for 20–25 minutes.
.....
Remove the pie from the oven and leave to rest for 10 minutes. Serve warm with ice cream or sorbet – don't worry if it's a bit messy to slice! If you prefer, you can refrigerate the pie and eat it cold too – it's just as delicious.

This is a super rich and indulgent tart. You don't need very much but I can guarantee you'll still want seconds!

MAKES A 36 X 12CM TART

Chocolate tart

750g milk chocolate,
   the best quality you
   can find, finely chopped
260ml double cream
120ml amaretto

For the pastry
175g plain flour, plus a
   little more for dusting
80g icing sugar
40g cocoa powder,
   70 per cent cocoa
   solids, the best quality
   you can find
140g butter, chilled and
   cut into small cubes
2 medium egg yolks,
   lightly beaten
2–3 tablespoons iced water

For the topping
200g whole blanched almonds
250g caster sugar
75g edible coffee beans
100g dark chocolate,
   70 per cent cocoa
   solids, grated

For the coffee cream
3 tablespoons coffee liqueur
1 tablespoon freeze-dried
   coffee granules, dissolved
   in 1 tablespoon boiling
   water and cooled
50g caster sugar
200ml double cream

To make the pastry, sift the flour, icing sugar and cocoa powder together into a bowl. Add the butter and rub together with your fingers until it has the consistency of breadcrumbs. Add the egg yolks and mix together gently with your fingers until it forms a soft paste. You may need to add a little iced water. Of course, you can do this in a food processor if you prefer. Wrap in cling film and place in the fridge to rest for at least 1 hour and up to a day.
.....
Preheat the oven to 170°C/Gas Mark 3.
.....
When you're ready to make the tart, roll out the pastry on a lightly floured surface into a rectangle about the thickness of a £1 coin. Line a 36 x 12cm loose-bottomed rectangular tart tin with the pastry, letting the excess fall over the sides. Line the inside with baking parchment or several layers of cling film and pour in some ceramic baking beans, uncooked rice or dried pulses to fill the base of the tart. Place the tart on a baking sheet and bake for 25 minutes. Remove from the oven, take out the parchment and beans and return to the oven to cook for a further 10–20 minutes until the tart shell is cooked through and dried out. Remove from the oven and cool, then trim the pastry to neaten the edges.
.....
To make the filling, place the chocolate in a heatproof bowl. Bring the double cream to the boil in a saucepan, pour on top of the chocolate and mix together until it has melted. Pour in the amaretto and mix thoroughly. If it isn't perfectly smooth, place the bowl on top of a pan of barely simmering water (the bottom of the bowl shouldn't touch the water) and stir until melted. Pour into the tart case and leave to cool at room temperature for 1 hour. Refrigerate for 30 minutes, or up to 2 days.
.....
Continues overleaf

Chocolate tart

Continued

Preheat the oven to 190°C/Gas Mark 5. To make the topping, place the almonds on a baking tray and cook for 8–10 minutes, until they are fragrant and lightly browned. Be careful not to burn them. Leave to cool.

.....

Put the caster sugar into a saucepan and warm over a medium heat until the sugar starts to colour. Add the almonds and stir until the sugar crystallises and coats the nuts. Tip on to a baking tray and cool.

.....

To make the coffee cream, mix together the coffee liqueur, dissolved coffee granules and the sugar in a large bowl. Pour on the double cream and whisk together until it thickens and forms lovely firm peaks, though be careful not to over whip it.

.....

Check that the tart has set. If not, you can leave it in the fridge for a further 20 minutes or so. Sprinkle on the edible coffee beans and then break up the frosted almonds and put them on top too. Cover with the grated chocolate and serve with the whipped coffee cream.

This cake is inspired by my mate Nicky Harvey. The only cooking she has ever done is a fridge cake but my god, she's very good at it! Next step, Nicky, is turning the oven on...

Caramel fridge cake

SERVES 8

150g dark muscovado sugar
150g butter
1 x 400ml tin caramel
Pinch of salt
300g dried sour cherries
50g caster sugar
Juice and freshly grated
    zest of 2 lemons
100ml cherry brandy

For the base
150g digestive biscuits
100g butter, melted
50g crisped rice cereal

For the milk chocolate topping
370ml milk
130ml double cream
6 egg yolks
50g caster sugar
400g milk chocolate, the
    best quality you can find,
    broken into small pieces

To serve
Some crème fraîche, whipped
A little grated chocolate
    (optional)

To make the base, whizz the digestive biscuits in a food processor until crushed. Pour in the butter and blitz together for a few seconds to mix, then scrape into a bowl and fold through the crisped rice cereal. Spread the mixture into the bottom of a 24cm loose-bottomed tart tin and flatten it out across the base and up the sides of the tin with the back of a metal spoon. Put the tin in the fridge to set for at least 1 hour, or overnight.

......

To make the caramel filling, stir the muscovado sugar and butter together in a saucepan over a gentle heat until the sugar dissolves. Pour in the caramel along with a pinch of salt and stir well. Remove from the heat and cool.

......

Put the dried sour cherries in a bowl and shake over the caster sugar and lemon zest. Bring the cherry brandy and lemon juice to the boil in a small saucepan then pour the liquid into the bowl so the cherries can absorb the liquid and soften. When cooled, drain the cherries and discard the liquid.

......

Take the tart base from the fridge, pour in the caramel and spread it evenly. Put the cherries on top and return to the fridge until it's firmed up and set – about 2 hours.

......

For the topping, bring the milk and cream to the boil in a saucepan. In a bowl, whisk together the egg yolks and sugar. Pour on the boiled milk and whisk together. Pour back into the pan and cook over a medium heat, stirring constantly, until the mix reaches 82°C on an instant-read thermometer or it coats the back of a wooden spoon.

......

Continues overleaf

Caramel fridge cake
Continued

Place the milk chocolate in a large mixing bowl, pour on the hot custard mixture through a fine sieve, and stir until the milk chocolate has melted and you have a thick mousse-like consistency. Leave it to cool for a couple of minutes and then spoon into the caramel and cherry tart. Spread the chocolate mixture out evenly and place the tart in the fridge to firm up for at least 2 hours or overnight. If you have any chocolate custard left over, pour it into a small cup and refrigerate until set – enjoy it as a little chocolate pot later.
.....
When you're ready to serve, remove the cake from the tin and serve with some whipped crème fraîche and a few gratings of chocolate to decorate, if you like.

These little individual cakes are really easy to make and you can cook them in ramekins, small ovenproof bowls or even in a large tin as one cake. There's no flour in the mixture, so they're quite velvety and rich. The orange and cardamom mascarpone adds extra notes of flavour and it really helps cut through the richness of the cakes.

Chocolate cakes with orange mascarpone

SERVES 6-8

For the cakes
190g dark chocolate,
    70 per cent cocoa solids,
    broken into small pieces
125g butter
4 eggs
190g caster sugar
Zest of 1 orange

For the mascarpone
75g mascarpone cheese
75ml double cream
Zest of ½ orange
6 cardamom pods,
    toasted lightly in a
    dry frying pan, seeds
    removed and crushed
25g caster sugar

Preheat the oven to 120°C/Gas Mark ½.
.....
Put the chocolate and butter into a large, heatproof bowl and place on top of a pan of barely simmering water – the bowl shouldn't touch the water – and melt together; stir until smooth.
.....
In a separate bowl, whisk together the eggs and sugar until light and fluffy. Take the bowl of melted chocolate from the heat, and whisk in the eggs and sugar. Add the orange zest and mix together. Divide this mix between six or eight small ovenproof bowls or ramekins, depending on their size, and bake for 45–50 minutes until they are just cooked – the mixture should still have a little wobble to it. Remove them from the oven and leave to cool a little.
.....
While they're cooling, whisk together all of the ingredients for the mascarpone cream until nice and smooth. Spoon a big dollop of this on top of the warm cakes and serve straight away.

basics

This flavour-packed stock base is made from chicken wings, a chicken carcass and a couple of pig's trotters. It can be used in any recipe that calls for chicken stock, or it can be reduced further to use as a meaty gravy (I serve it as a gravy to accompany the Pork fillet patties with bubble and squeak on page 170).

Meat stock base

MAKES ABOUT 7.5 LITRES

1kg chicken wings
2 pig's trotters, cut in
   half lengthways (ask the
   butcher to do this for you
   if you don't have a cleaver)
1kg chicken carcass, chopped
4 celery sticks, cut in half
1 onion, chopped
1 garlic bulb, unpeeled, but
   cut in half horizontally
200g tinned tomatoes
10 litres water

Preheat the oven to 180°C/Gas Mark 4. Put the chicken wings in a large roasting tray and roast for about 30 minutes until dark golden brown. Make sure they don't burn.

.....

Transfer the wings to a large saucepan. Add the trotters, chicken carcass, celery, onion and garlic. Pour in the tomatoes and the water and bring to the boil, skimming the surface as necessary. Reduce the heat to very low and leave the stock to simmer, uncovered, for 6–8 hours, until reduced by one quarter.

.....

Pass the stock through a fine sieve lined with muslin or a clean tea towel. Leave to cool completely, then transfer to the fridge for 12 hours so that any fat will set and can be removed.

.....

This recipe makes a large quantity but it will keep for up to 3 days in the fridge. Alternatively, measure it out into 200ml freezer bags and freeze until needed – it will last for up to 3 months.

You might be wondering how this chicken stock differs from the meat stock base opposite, when the ingredients are so similar, but simmering additional roasted chicken wings in the liquid gives this recipe an extra layer of deep flavour. It can be used as a cooking liquor but I generally reduce it further to use as a thick base for stews and pies.

Rich chicken stock

MAKES ABOUT 2 LITRES

2kg chicken wings
3 litres Meat stock base
  (see opposite)
Salt

Preheat the oven to 180°C/Gas Mark 4. Put the chicken wings in a roasting tray and roast for about 30 minutes until dark golden brown. Make sure they don't burn.

.....

Transfer the wings to a large saucepan, cover with the meat stock base and bring to the boil. Reduce the heat to very low and leave to simmer, uncovered, until reduced by one third. Season with salt and pass through a sieve lined with muslin or a clean tea towel. Leave to cool completely, then cover and chill for 12 hours so that any fat will set and can be removed.

.....

The stock will keep in the fridge for 3 days, or you can measure it out into 200ml freezer bags and freeze until needed – it will last for up to 3 months.

Chicken gravy

MAKES ABOUT 1 LITRE

Vegetable oil, for cooking
400g turkey leg meat,
  skin on, diced
1 tablespoon runny honey
2 tablespoons dark soy sauce
30g butter
30g plain flour
1 litre Rich chicken stock
  (see above), warm
Salt

Heat a little oil in a large saucepan and add the diced turkey meat. Fry until you get an even golden brown colour all over and the skin has gone crisp. Add the honey and soy sauce to the pan and cook for a further 2–3 minutes. Add the butter and, when melted, add the flour and stir, making sure that the turkey gets a good covering. Slowly add the warm chicken stock, stirring constantly.

.....

When all of the stock has been added, bring the sauce to the boil. Reduce to a simmer and cook for 25–30 minutes, stirring frequently, until the gravy is thick.

.....

Season with salt then pass through a fine sieve. The gravy can be kept in the fridge for 3 days, or you can measure it out into 200ml freezer bags and freeze until needed – it will last for up to 3 months.

Pork stock

MAKES ABOUT 1.25 LITRES

1.5kg pork bones, chopped (ask your butcher to do this for you if you don't have a cleaver)
1.5 litres Rich chicken stock (see p. 285)
3 sage leaves

Preheat the oven to 180°C/Gas Mark 4. Place the pork bones in a large roasting tray and roast for about 40 minutes until a deep auburn colour, then drain off any excess fat.

.....

Put the bones into a large saucepan, cover with the chicken stock and bring to the boil. Reduce the heat and simmer until the stock has reduced by half, skimming off any fat every 15 minutes. Add the sage leaves, turn off the heat and leave to infuse for 5 minutes. Pass through a fine sieve. Cover and put in the fridge for 12 hours so that any fat will set and can be removed.

.....

The stock will keep in the fridge for 3 days, or you can measure it out into 200ml freezer bags and freeze until needed – it will last for up to 3 months.

Ham stock

MAKES ABOUT 1.25 LITRES

1.3kg ham bones or gammon or smoked bacon rind
1 onion, roughly chopped
1 celery stick, roughly chopped
3 bay leaves
1 star anise
4 parsley stalks

Place the bones in a large saucepan and cover with cold water. Bring the water to the boil, skim off any scum that comes to the top, then add the vegetables, bay leaves and star anise. Simmer for 1 hour, then remove from the heat, add the parsley stalks and leave to infuse until the stock is cool. Pass through a fine sieve. Cover and put in the fridge for 12 hours so that any fat will set and can be removed.

.....

The stock will keep in the fridge for 3 days, or you can measure it out into 200ml freezer bags and freeze until needed – it will last for up to 3 months.

Lamb stock

1kg lamb bones, chopped (ask your butcher to do this for you if you don't have a cleaver)

2 litres Meat stock base (see p. 284)

5–6 rosemary sprigs

Preheat the oven to 180°C/Gas Mark 4. Put the lamb bones in a large roasting tray and roast for about 40 minutes until dark golden brown. Transfer them to a saucepan placed over a very low heat with the meat stock base and leave to simmer for 4–6 hours until the quantity reduces by half.
.....

Remove the pan from the heat, add the rosemary and leave to infuse, uncovered, for 30 minutes.
.....

Pass the stock through a fine sieve lined with muslin. Leave to cool completely, then cover and put in the fridge for 12 hours so that any fat will set and can be removed.
.....

This stock is now ready to use, or it can be reduced further to use as a sauce. It will keep in the fridge for 3 days, or you can measure it out into 200ml freezer bags and freeze until needed – it will last for up to 3 months.

Beef stock

100ml rapeseed oil
400g beef trimmings
2 litres chicken stock
4 star anise
6–8 thyme sprigs
1 garlic bulb, unpeeled but
   cut in half horizontally
Salt

Heat the rapeseed oil in a large saucepan over a high heat. Add the beef trimmings and fry them, stirring occasionally, until browned and almost burnt, but definitely not burnt! Add the chicken stock and star anise and bring to the boil. Add the thyme and garlic.

. . . . .

Reduce the heat to very low and leave to simmer, uncovered, for 2 hours, or until the stock has reduced by one third. Season with salt and pass the stock through a sieve lined with muslin. Leave to cool completely, then cover and chill for 12 hours so any fat will set and can be removed.

. . . . .

The stock is now ready to use, or it can be reduced further to use as a sauce. It will keep for up to 3 days in the fridge, or you can measure it out into 200ml freezer bags and freeze until needed – it will last for up to 3 months.

Beef gravy

1.5kg beef, duck, lamb or
venison bones (basically
any red meat bones will do),
chopped quite small (ask
your butcher to do this
for you if you don't have
a cleaver)

1 pig's trotter, split lengthways
(ask the butcher to do this
for you if you don't have
a cleaver)

2.5 litres Meat stock base
(see p. 284)

375ml red wine

2 tablespoons redcurrant jelly

1 bunch of flat-leaf parsley,
tied together

1 tablespoon cornflour
(optional)

Salt

The day before you are going to use the gravy, preheat the oven
to 200°C/Gas Mark 6 and put the bones in a large roasting tray.
Put the tray in the oven and roast the bones for 30 minutes,
or until dark brown but not burnt.
.....

Transfer the bones to a large saucepan placed over a high heat.
Add the pig's trotter, meat stock base, red wine and redcurrant
jelly and bring to the boil, stirring to dissolve the jelly. Use a large
metal spoon to skim any scum from the surface, as necessary.
Reduce the heat to very low and leave to simmer, uncovered,
for 3 hours, or until the liquid has reduced by one third.
.....

Turn the heat off, add the parsley – stalks and all – and leave to
infuse, uncovered, for 10 minutes. Pass the gravy through a fine
sieve into a bowl, then leave to cool completely. Cover and place
in the fridge for 12 hours so any fat will set and can be removed.
.....

When you're ready to use, remove and discard the fat. Pour the
gravy into a saucepan and bring to the boil. If you want your gravy
a little thicker, blend the cornflour with 1 tablespoon of the sauce,
then pour it into the pan and continue simmering, whisking
vigorously, until it has thickened. Season with salt, then pass the
gravy through a sieve lined with muslin and it's ready to serve.
.....

The gravy can be kept in the fridge for 3 days, or you can measure
it out into 200ml freezer bags and freeze until needed – it will
last for up to 3 months.

Red wine sauce

MAKES ABOUT 900ML

2 litres Meat stock base
(see p. 284)
750ml red wine
150g redcurrant jelly
100g frozen blackberries
1 onion, chopped
4 celery sticks, chopped
Handful of parsley stalks
Salt and freshly ground
black pepper

Mix the meat stock base, wine, redcurrant jelly and blackberries together in a saucepan over a high heat and bring to the boil, stirring to dissolve the jelly. Add the onion and celery and continue boiling until it reduces down to one third of its original volume, skimming the surface as necessary.

......

Remove the pan from the heat, add the parsley stalks and leave to infuse, uncovered, for 10 minutes. Pass the liquid through a sieve lined with muslin and leave to cool completely. Cover and chill for 12 hours so that any fat will set and can be removed.

......

After you remove the fat, place the liquid over a medium heat and leave it to bubble, uncovered, for about 25 minutes until it reduces to a sauce consistency. Season with salt and black pepper.

......

The sauce can be kept in the fridge for 3 days, or you can measure it out into 200ml freezer bags and freeze until needed – it will last for up to 3 months.

Curry powder

MAKES ABOUT 120G

2 tablespoons ground chilli
2 tablespoons ground ginger
2 tablespoons garam masala
1 tablespoon ground star anise
1 tablespoon cardamom seeds
1 tablespoon coriander seeds
1 tablespoon cumin seeds
1 tablespoon black
onion seeds
1 tablespoon yellow
mustard seeds
1 tablespoon whole
black peppercorns
½ cinnamon stick

Preheat the oven to 180°C/Gas Mark 4. Mix all the spices together in a baking tray. Place the tray in the oven and roast for 10 minutes. Remove the tray from the oven and stir, then return it to the oven and roast for a further 4–5 minutes until the spices look and smell toasted, but not burnt! Immediately tip the spices out of the tray and leave to cool.

......

Grind the spices to a powder in a spice grinder or with a pestle and mortar, then sift through a fine sieve to give an even finer powder. Store in an airtight container until needed. It will keep for up to 3 months.

Pickle liquor

MAKES ABOUT 1.5 LITRES

1 litre white wine vinegar
250ml water
500g caster sugar
5 star anise
2 cloves
1 cinnamon stick
2 tablespoons white
    peppercorns
1 tablespoon coriander seeds
1 tablespoon fennel seeds

Put all the ingredients in a large saucepan over a high heat and bring to the boil, stirring to dissolve the sugar. Reduce the heat to low and leave the mix to simmer, uncovered, for 10–15 minutes.
.....
Remove the pan from the heat and cover the top with cling film or a tight-fitting lid, then leave to infuse and cool completely.
.....
Pass the mix through a fine sieve, then store in a non-metallic sealed container in the fridge. It will keep for up to 1 month.

Onion jam

MAKES ABOUT 450G

1.5kg Spanish onions, halved
    and finely sliced
50g demerara sugar
2 garlic cloves, grated
120ml water
100ml cider vinegar
½ tablespoon thyme leaves

Place the onions in a large, heavy-bottomed, non-stick saucepan. Add the sugar, garlic, water and cider vinegar. Cook over a medium heat, stirring to dissolve the sugar. Continue to stir at frequent intervals until the jam is thick, brown and sticky – this will take up to 1 hour.
.....
Remove from the heat and cool. When cold, stir in the thyme. Seal in a sterilised jar or container (see p. 39 for sterilising instructions). It will keep for up to a week in the fridge.

index

acknowledgements

A massive thank you to all who work with Absolute Press and Bloomsbury Publishing, with a particular salute to the great Jon Croft for taking the punt on us, Natalie Bellos, Xa Shaw Stewart and the fantastic Debora Robertson, who made the writing of this book a lot less painful than pulling out teeth with a set of rusty pliers. Love you guys! And thanks also to Marina Asenjo and Imogen Fortes, for their production and editing expertise.

For the design of the book, huge appreciation goes out to Emma and Alex at Smith & Gilmour. I'd like to thank Alex for his help with the vision and the creative side, especially for tasting all the food (you did a great job of that, chief!).

Thanks so much to all the great team at Outline Productions for putting together yet another visually stunning, fun-to-make, and information-full cookery show. So many of you to mention, but just a few names: Bridget Boseley, Sarah Myland, Sally Wingate, Richard Hill, Robbie 'the power-hammer' Johnson, Conor Connolly, Archie Thomas, Polly Huntingford, Anne Bos, Ella Taylor, Elaine Byfield, Tim Leask, Rob Beck and anybody else who worked on the show who I can't fit in here. I can't thank you guys enough!

Big thank you to the BBC for the support that they have shown me and the great solid food that this country is built on. I love being part of the family; thanks for inviting me along, Alison Kirkham and Lindsay Bradbury.

And then a huge thank you to everybody in my life who is involved in food and The Hand & Flowers, starting with my dream team of Lourdes Dooley and Aaron Mulliss, and then all the super-chefs who worked on the book: Chris Mackett, Nick Beardshaw, Jamie May, Luke Henderson, Robin 'Haggis' McCrindle, Freddie Cook and Ben Hobson. Also, the pretty girls – Victoria Bucknall and Jessica Mills.

To the two lovely ladies who really did make this book come to life, the ever dependable, unflustered and rock-solid Alex Longstaff, and, with her amazing high energy and bounce, Nicole Herft. Without you two, this book wouldn't even be halfway finished by now. I'm pretty sure there would be many more spelling mistakes and I wouldn't have ordered enough food for the photographs! Big love to you two!

And I must say a massive thank you to the people helping guide us through this crazy world, the 'super' Borra Garson and her trusty sidekick Louise Leftwich, and the incredible, pink-champagne-drinking Zoe Wilmer and Amy Williams.

Finally, to the greatest non-meat eater I know, a man who makes magic happen and things look lovely, 'the wizard' Cristian Barnett and his lovely assistant, Brid. Thank you guys so much for persevering and redoing that treacle tart shoot again and again...

To anybody else who I have forgotten – I'm sure there are many, because unbeknown to you lot, the members of the book-buying community, so many people are involved in making this happen – thank you all so much.

Massive love and hugs,
Big Tom

First published in Great Britain
in 2014 by Absolute Press, an imprint
of Bloomsbury Publishing Plc

Tom Kerridge's Best Ever Dishes is an Outline
production for BBC TWO.

Absolute Press
Scarborough House
29 James Street West
Bath BA1 2BT
Phone 44 (0) 1225 316013
Fax 44 (0) 1225 445836
Email office@absolutepress.co.uk
Website absolutepress.co.uk

Bloomsbury Publishing Plc
50 Bedford Square
London WC1B 3DP

Bloomsbury is a trademark
of Bloomsbury Publishing Plc.

Bloomsbury Publishing, London,
New Delhi, New York and Sydney

bloomsbury.com

A CIP record for this book is available
from the British Library.

ISBN 978 1 4729 0941 1

10 9 8 7 6 5 4 3 2 1

Project editor: Imogen Fortes

Design and art direction: Smith & Gilmour

Photographer: Cristian Barnett, crisbarnett.com

Food editor: Debora Robertson

Food stylists: Tom Kerridge, Nicole Herft
and Aaron Mulliss

Prop stylists: Polly Webb-Wilson
and Tamzin Ferdinando

Cover calligraphy: Peter Horridge, horridge.com

Indexer: Lisa Footitt

Printed in Italy by Graphicom

A note about the text: This book has been
typeset in Sentinel, one of many descendants
of the Clarendon font, a slab-serif first
introduced in 1845.